NEW WAYS TO BETTER MEETINGS

New Ways to
Better Meetings

REVISED, ENLARGED EDITION

BERT AND FRANCES STRAUSS

Drawings by Thomas E. Hutchens

NEW YORK · THE VIKING PRESS

First published in 1951
Revised edition first published in 1964 by
The Viking Press, Inc., 625 Madison Avenue, New York, N.Y. 10022

Published simultaneously in Canada by
The Macmillan Company of Canada Limited

Library of Congress catalog card number: 64-23156
Printed in the U.S.A. by the Vail-Ballou Press, Inc.

Second printing November 1966

FOREWORD

About fifteen years ago we wrote the earlier version of this book to explain to the general reader the ways—then very new indeed—which the social scientists had evolved to help people work together more effectively in groups. It was originally published in 1951, at a time when the meetings it described were, to many readers, startlingly different from those they had been attending.

Since then, there has been a steadily growing acceptance of the ideas it contained, as well as an extraordinary advance in both related research and practice. In 1947, for example, when the National Training Laboratories held its first summer session at Bethel, Maine, only a handful of trainers were present. Fifteen years later over a hundred were required. In that span of time over four thousand people had attended the laboratories and some six thousand others, largely executives and managers, had attended sessions elsewhere. In the United States nine regional centers were formed and thirty-four universities undertook experimental research on the subject. Exploration is now also going on widely in Europe and has begun in Latin America and Asia.

More and more industries as well as government agencies have found it rewarding to take into account the findings of the social scientists on how workers respond to each other in group situations. Thirty-three companies—more than half of them ranking among the country's best "blue-chip" producers—make grants to the Foundation for Research in Human Behavior in Michigan, which brings together businessmen and social scientists to plan research and consider how its findings affect management problems.

The time seemed right, therefore, to look back over what we said

v

fifteen years ago, to decide what needed to be changed and added. In doing so we found that subsequent research actually made us wish to change very little in the "how-to" of the new ways. They still provide the setting, the framework, and the climate for better meetings, whether those meetings take place in the neighborhood school or in some industrial plant. Where we have made changes, it has been in the hope of clarifying some process for the reader.

What we have added is a new section to show how meetings which share the thinking of all the members can help create better functioning in multi-level organizations.

BERT AND FRANCES STRAUSS

CONTENTS

CONTENTS

NEW WAYS TO BETTER MEETINGS

1: MEMBER-CENTERED MEETINGS

1. WHAT IT'S ALL ABOUT

This book is for anyone who has to lead meetings, large or small, and has an uneasy feeling that they aren't what they might be. It is also for those less happily situated, who have to go to those meetings and would be the first to admit that most of them are a bore, an irritation, or sheer waste of time.

For some years now, ideas have come marching across the mental horizon which, rightly applied, can change the picture for both leaders and the so-called led. They have resulted in a new type of meeting, often called "member-centered," because its focus is on what *all* those present want to accomplish. These ideas have emerged from the experiments and tests which social scientists have been making in a particular field of human relations: how people affect one another when they come together in a group. Each person present, they reasoned, was trying to influence that group in some way; he was therefore a force in it. What these forces do to one another, and how, and why, was the starting point in their research, and continues to be the subject of intensive and growing research.

We all pay lip service to the notion, as old as that of democracy, that a group, as a group, can solve its problems better than an individual. The social scientists have made it possible to turn that lip service into action. They offer practical ways to pull together the forces within a group and help it solve its problems creatively by using all the ability and experience its members possess.

For members these new methods have an effect roughly comparable to a shot of adrenalin. They feel a kind of personal possession, responsibility, and eagerness about the group's problems which they had not known before. Having really shared in making decisions,

Captive . . . without a chance of talking back

they want to share in carrying them out. The helpless sense of being captive to boredom and tedium, of being talked at without a chance of talking back, can be lessened and often eliminated, even in a large meeting or conference.

For a leader, the use of these new methods offers a great relief. The success or failure of the committee does not rest on his shoulders alone. The burden is divided. His job is no longer the tense one of pushing and cajoling, with part of his mind always concerned for his reputation as a chairman.

For the group's purpose, working along these lines produces a marked change in results, both during and after the sessions. Most traditional meetings turn into a debate among the articulate few. Their ideas and personalities stick up—to use the old simile—like the peak of an iceberg. But this new kind of meeting allows the submerged intelligence and skill of the other members to come to the surface, where they can be used.

Night after night, all over the country, the cars stream out—to PTA meetings, to Emergency School meetings, to church and civic meetings. They go to management societies, to club groups, to boards of Community Chest, Camp Fire Girls, Scouts—to an endless and varied number of meetings. And day after day there are staff conferences or training programs or supervisors holding meetings for their staffs. Management meets with labor; foremen meet in conference with workers. Committees shape the activities of large national associations and clubs hold regional or country-wide meetings. All up and down the line people come together in a wholehearted if sometimes not very effective effort to share problems.

There is, in fact, an enormous amount of good will and desire to help. We are now able to draw on it with an effectiveness lacking before. For we have never before had a working method by which all the ability represented in a group could be expressed and focused. Without working techniques to bolster our good will, we bungled in our efforts to use it. We had plans and decisions "explained" by those at the top rather than any shared progress toward those plans and decisions. All this is changing with remarkable rapidity as people learn that these difficulties can be avoided. But most of us are still the captives of old meeting habits.

Back in 1876 an "eminent engineer" took stock in his orderly mind of all the facts he had read and noted and studied for years about parliamentary procedure. It occurred to him that he could make good use of that interest by writing a book to systematize that procedure. His name was Henry Martyn Robert and he called his book *Robert's Rules of Order*. He made very good use of his interest indeed. In no time his book had sold over a million copies.

From then until the new insight of the social scientists became public knowledge, we were hedged in by the rules Mr. Robert compiled. There is no doubt that they are convenient and orderly. In many cases they are necessary.

There is no question, however, that *Robert's Rules* limit the creativity of groups which want to solve problems or carry on action programs. They make it possible for a few to take control and impose their convictions on those others not quite so ready to spring to their feet, not quite so able to phrase emphatically what they want to say. They force the role of boss—or dictator—on the chairman. They set such a rigid pattern for the usual meeting that although the members go, from duty or necessity, many of them won't bother to take an active part in it.

We now know (and research continues to emphasize) that participation, and only participation, will release the untapped supply of

4 NEW WAYS TO BETTER MEETINGS

energy and ideas. Industries have discovered that it results in greater production, cuts down on absenteeism, and provides a real incentive to better the product, whatever it may be. In any organization or group, the situation is comparable. When the members are allowed to build with those at the top, the whole enterprise picks up new energy. It makes little difference whether these members are paid for their services or are volunteering them; whether one talks in terms of man-hours lost or mind-hours. The salvaging of time and energy is the same.

But it was not until the social scientists turned their attention to groups that we began to struggle out from under the dead hand of habit and Mr. Robert's rules.

In the late thirties Ronald Lippitt, a graduate student at the University of Iowa, spotted the word "groups" in a list of possible subjects for a Ph.D. thesis. He tracked down the professor responsible for the suggested subject, the brilliant Viennese social psychologist Kurt Lewin, and one of the most fruitful collaborations in the whole field of the social sciences began.

The work which they did in that pupil-teacher relationship was of the kind that suddenly opens a door to a new area of research. It was not that the door labeled "groups" had been closed before. Plenty of research had gone on, but it had been along other lines. Lewin and Lippitt found new ways to spotlight human beings in groups.* The initial experiments were to determine what different kinds of leaders did to the groups working under them.

In one of these experiments four boys' clubs were organized to work on similar projects but under different kinds of leaders: the boss or policeman type; the laissez-faire or good-fellow, noninterfering type; and the democratic type. The two social scientists devised methods to analyze what went on in the meetings and used all possible statistical and scientific checks to make sure there would be no loopholes in the findings.

The boys were eleven years old, as nearly alike as could be found in background, interests, intelligence, skill, and so on. The groups met in the same place at different times. Not only did they work under different types of leaders, but from time to time leaders were

---

* Ronald Lippitt and Ralph K. White, "An Experimental Study of Leadership and Group Life," summarized in *Readings in Social Psychology*, edited by Maccoby, Newcomb, and Hartley (New York: Henry Holt, 1958).

interchanged. On certain occasions the leaders failed to appear or were late. When this happened, a janitor or some other outsider walked in, surveyed what the boys were making, pointed out mistakes, and made himself as obnoxious as he could.

When an outsider walked in on the group with the policeman type of leader, he so upset its members that they turned on one of the boys and made a scapegoat of him. These boys, in the absence of their leader, were baffled, unable to continue with their work, and went generally to pieces as a group.

Those who operated under the lenient hand of the good-fellow leader showed the greatest development in knowledge, having had to work things out for themselves. But they were well behind the others in accomplishment. They also spent a good deal of their time making life miserable for a few victims, particularly when the outsider came in to annoy them.

When the democratic leader walked out on his group, the boys went right on working. They did not pick on one another. When the critical stranger came in they got angry, thoroughly angry. But instead of taking out their anger on one of the group, they turned on the stranger or, in one instance, took their hammers and chisels and smashed some plywood stacked nearby for their use. In fact, they acted with considerable maturity for eleven-year-olds.

These experiments (not nearly so simple as they sound in this quick telling) gave additional push to research which has since gathered in its wake a steadily increasing number of educators, sociologists, anthropologists, and psychologists. It was a dynamic approach to the conception that human beings can be studied as elements. What makes a group click? What makes it disintegrate? What do people do to one another when they get into a group? Why do we often surprise ourselves in a group? What kind of chain reaction does this getting together set up? Is a group a thing in itself, different from the individuals who make it up? Is one group remarkably like any other?

Research on the subject continues, spreading out from such fields as group dynamics, sociometry, cultural anthropology, and sociodrama. But to date the findings do not contradict the early creative conclusion, that under similar conditions groups do act remarkably like one another. The things that are wrong with them are pretty much the same too—and so are the cures.

What makes a group click?

Member-centered meetings are one of the ways in which we have benefited from that research, from which some of the material in this book stems directly. Other parts of it come from experience obtained by making practical application of the research results. A third major source has been that of the devices developed and successfully used for training groups or for helping groups to improve themselves.

In the first part of what follows, we have used community groups as a background for tracing how the methods can be used. Later we have tried to show the helpfulness of these methods at strategic points in the management of large organizations. In whatever setting, the value of member-centered meetings is that they tap the resources of the people who have come together.

II: USE IN COMMUNITY GROUPS

2. WHAT'S WRONG WITH OUR MEETINGS

Once we had a committee.

"Will you come next Tuesday night," we asked, "to talk about the school situation?"

Yes, they would come. They would all come. We called the local funeral parlor to rent chairs; we pushed back the furniture in the living room to make space. Still more people, hearing about the meeting, came.

There were the usual officers: chairman, secretary, treasurer.

"Would a dollar-fifty dues per year be too much?"

"It's not enough. There's too much to be done. Make it more."

For three Tuesday evenings we met with energy and eagerness. At the fourth we agreed we must have a constitution and bylaws. A subcommittee was appointed to prepare them. The next meeting was devoted to going over their work, paragraph by paragraph. Then, as Mr. X kept breaking in with, "You can't do that—it won't be legal," we began going over those pages almost word by word.

Fewer and fewer people came. Finally there was the Tuesday when we decided we no longer needed to rent extra chairs. Then even our own remained unfilled.

"What's the matter? What happened?" we kept asking.

Then there is what might be called the Railroaded Committee.

Once a month this committee meets to work out a training program which is to be handed on to volunteer leaders. The members are intelligent, hard-working, and by all odds better and more efficient than the average meeting-goer. They get down to work promptly; they end promptly. During the meeting they give most of their attention to the job at hand. The chairman is charming, tactful, and competent.

But there was the occasion, early in the year's meetings, when the committee got stuck on the real nature of their job: were they themselves to do the training, or were they to supply it from more skilled sources? The argument went back and forth, with considerable feeling on both sides.

Suddenly there was a pause and the chairman broke in, "Then we're agreed that we will do the actual training?"

The members were not agreed, but the old habit of deference to authority held. They argued no more. Once in the hall outside, however, the resentment of the unconvinced burst forth.

Then there are the committees that might be labeled Lambs-to-Slaughter.

These are the groups made up of people who don't know what they're coming together for. They sit, waiting to be told. In communities, in business, in industry, in trade and professional associations, in so-called "training" situations, busy people will sit politely for two or three hours, listening to a series of speeches. These may be good or bad—but the members, or audience, are powerless to do anything about it, one way or another.

The weekly staff meeting falls into this category. Each member doodles on the pad of paper which lies at his place. He waits to get a cue from the boss as to how much he dares to say and what. Should the boss be the kind who encourages free talk from his subordinates, that helps. But usually the staff is there to be told, at endless length. For a time they listen. Then they begin to glance at their watches: will their lunch dates wait half an hour, forty-five minutes? Will he never get through talking?

Many different types of "sick" groups could be described, but everyone can furnish examples from his own experience. More to the point is to ask why they are sick. What's wrong with many of the meetings all of us go to? What happens? Why do these meetings fall completely short of what they might accomplish, both during and after the meeting? The reason is almost always the same, although it comes about in different ways: the members have lost the desire to participate. It has been killed, one way or another.

In the Lambs-to-Slaughter kind of group, it rarely has a chance even to come to birth. In our school committee we killed it ourselves, without realizing what we were doing, by grinding out a constitution and bylaws. We killed it with boredom. In the Railroaded group it was done by suppression. Whenever a few members gather resentfully in the hall after a small meeting, they have just left a "sick" group. No one likes to have his convictions ignored and overruled. If what he says isn't going to be treated for what it's worth, why should he bother to say it? For that matter, why should he bother to go to the meeting?

Neither the chairman nor the office boss is to be blamed for this lack of participation. Nor are the members. Until new methods are used to change old attitudes and divide responsibility among participants, meetings will stay sick.

Every group is different

"But My Group Is Different!"

Quite right. Every group is different. Even the same group becomes different when a new member replaces an old one. A group acts one way at tonight's meeting and quite another way at next week's, when it is working on another problem and the members are feeling different.

Whether the group produces much or little depends on the type of behavior members fall into, often unintentionally. One man who is always on the ball may take over five meetings in a row, dominating and running them as only he can. At the sixth meeting he fails to appear. Everything seems changed. "Best meeting we ever had," someone comments when it is over, "the whole meeting felt different." But the truth is that this member enjoyed the meeting so much because he at last got his innings; he did the dominating.

The group changes because the behavior patterns in it change. Everyone is aware of the subtle shifting of attitude in a group when a new member turns up. But it is a change of emphasis or of degree. The same patterns of behavior are still there at every meeting and in every group, including those that hinder it, by interrupting or distracting, and sometimes bringing it to a complete halt.

One of the first steps toward making a meeting productive is to recognize the following roles. All of us have been guilty of assuming one or more of them in meetings. There are many, but here are the most familiar ones, divided into Nuisance and Destructive types. And though we describe each of these as though describing a member, that is only to make them more easily recognizable. What follows should be read in terms of activities any member is likely to exhibit at one time or another.

Nuisance Types

Pigeonholer

Also might be called the get-it-in-the-notebook member. All through the meeting he's busy indenting 1 under A. He carries small notebooks with him for this purpose. He hardly hears what's going on because his mind is on these notes. What he will ever make of them is a secret—from him too.

Hair-splitter

Too orderly minded type. Can't function unless he has definitions. Everything has to be named, labeled, and packaged. First cousin to the Pigeonholer.

Eager Beaver

Wide-eyed enthusiast. "This just occurred to me . . . I haven't thought it out yet, but . . ."

Explorer

Kin to Eager Beaver. Every new plan or idea excites this member, whether or not he's known anything about it before, or knows anything about it now.

Talker

Member of a large family, some of whom have graduated from the Nuisance into the Destructive class. Our favorite is the modest one who always manages to explain how "I just happen to have made a special study of that, and I think I can help you out. . . ." And he does, forever and ever.

Fence-sitter

Or bandwagon jumper. This member never commits himself until all the returns are in. Then he becomes conspicuously in favor of

the winning verdict. In an office he waits for a cue from the boss.

Superior Being

Looks down his nose at the whole affair. Studies fingernails throughout meeting. Noncommittal, nonparticipating. Doesn't want to be bothered. He came because his good friend Blank just insisted . . .

Doubting Thomas

The head-shaker, the "I-don't-think-it-can-possibly-work" type. Akin to "I-don't-think-they'll-like-it" type.

Wisecracker

Fancies himself as the group clown, that needed "light touch." Brags, tells stories, always thinks of "a good one you ought to hear —fits right in with what we're talking about."

Depreciator

"Of course I know you are all smarter than I am and have more experience. So what I have to say probably isn't very important and won't interest you, but . . ."

Destructive Types

(We admit that the line between Nuisance and downright Destructive types is hard to draw. Scratch one and you're likely to find the other.)

Dominator

Ten minutes of a meeting are enough to get him to take off his velvet glove. Monopolizes discussion, gives orders, dictates. Tries to be patient with the slow reactions of the others—but not for long. The boss type.

Or there is the other kind of dominator, who thinks faster, has more facts, is honestly way out ahead of the others.

Manipulator

Flatters other members by open, special praise during the meeting, or seeks members out afterward: "Say, I thought you had a very special point there. They should have been paying more attention to you. . . ." Starts little cliques or subgroups.

Belittler

Always criticizes or ignores other members. Gives an acid edge even to the best-intended remark.

Always Vulnerable

Interprets every disagreement as a personal attack. Wastes group's time defending himself and explaining. Much later will come back to it by saying, "That's exactly what I meant when I said . . ."

Blocker

The mule. Goes farther than the Doubting Thomas. He not only doubts, he balks. It takes a major fire to get him to move. He doesn't give reasons. He thinks his one solution is best and won't give it up. If the meeting has moved on, he'll break in and make it go back to his point.

Distractor

Refuses to get down to business. Cuts in with inconsequentials. Leads group off subject. Whispers to member on left or right.

Besides Nuisance and Destructive types, there is another problem category, the Silent Members, who are discussed in Chapter 12.

Any chairman can furnish one example after another of problem members. His customary handling of them is to suppress them. He controls the meeting. He has a bag of tricks to help him cope with Nuisance, Destructive, or Silent Members. And he is rated tops among chairmen if he can do this suppressing job with a high degree of politeness and charm.

The scientists have found a better way. They have found how to channel these destructive forces into constructive ones, how to employ the same energy to enrich and organize group thinking. But change cannot be made without changing the mechanism and spirit of the meeting itself, any more than one can kill bacteria without changing the culture in which they grow.

3. ONCE OVER LIGHTLY

Let us assume, for the moment, that you are the chairman of a small group. Or, when next September rolls around, you will be. Maybe it is the local school board or a committee of the Scouts in your neighborhood; perhaps it is a group formed in your church or office. In any case, having considerable pride about that group, you would like to make a success of it.

You have heard somewhere that there are new ways for groups to work together through which, at long last, the responsibility of the leader is actually shared by the members; through which a decision can be reached without voting and without *Robert's Rules of Order.* The possibility sounds interesting but utopian, and you are a practical man.

Research may be all right for the social scientists, but they don't have your group on their hands. They don't have to come down hard on Joe Ellison, week after week, to keep him from running the show. They don't have to put up with that little Mrs. Buck, wasting everyone's time while she finds a mental pigeonhole for every statement; or with Hortense Nelson, who never stops talking; or Andrew Mack, who never begins. They don't have to remember all the personal likes and dislikes and arguments, and try to straighten them out. If the chairman doesn't run things, who will? If there are no votes, how will the group ever make a decision?

Although you are willing to tackle anything that promises more successful meetings, you would like a once-over-lightly on the general subject before going on with details. So here is a brief picture of a "member-centered" meeting. The key to it, as we've said before, lies in a shift of attitude on the part of both leader and members, with changed methods to reinforce—indeed, to help create—the shift.

At tonight's meeting all the same people are there (your neighbors and ours), all the difficult ones and all the articulate ones— Joe Ellison, Mrs. Buck, Hortense Nelson, even Andrew Mack, and a number of others. They are still recognizable, but they are behaving differently.

There are only fifteen people present (ten or twelve would be an even better number; too many people tend to split up into more than one group). They are sitting in a U-shaped group around a table, as groups usually do when they have a table large enough. But the open end of the U is occupied not by a chairman, but by a large blackboard, or an easel with a pad of big sheets of paper.

Less time than usual is wasted in getting this meeting down to business. (Only in heaven would no time be wasted.) Before the very first of these new meetings took place the participants filled in a "problem census," saying what they thought the main job of the group should be. At the first meeting they agreed on the general goal. At the end of each session thereafter they decided which phase of the general problem they would discuss at the next, so they don't have to follow a chairman's agenda or wait for him to say, "I thought tonight we would talk about . . ."

Indeed, the chairman as we have known him in the past has departed along with his agenda. The leader sits at the table on a par with the others, a symbol that he has exchanged his old position

That familiar troublemaking look

as boss of the group for an even more valuable one: its stimulator. He opens the meeting. He is distinctly its leader, but his job is not to control; it is to help all the members contribute to the solving of the group's problem. And the members' job is to share his.

The meeting proceeds with a degree of informality which would make Mr. Robert turn over in his grave. Not only do the members call one another by their first names (a detail, but one which usually promotes closeness and greater freedom), but they have a kind of first-name attitude toward each other. They all—and particularly the leader—turn facts, points in discussion, and suggestions into questions which are thrown out in a general way to the whole group, not to an individual.

Instead of cutting off argument or controlling it, the leader and the others deliberately try to get all points of view out in the open. That look on one member's face—for instance, that familiar, troublemaking look—which they used to try to ignore, they now hunt for.

With the knowledge that if a member gets rid of whatever he resents now he will be the readier to make a positive contribution, they try to find out what's on his mind.

The members and leader share another job, too: that of focusing the discussion. Even the best group is made up of human beings whose normal equipment seems to include a tendency to wander off the subject. But in this meeting the members' shared responsibility helps channel the talk. Besides, they have specific aids to help keep that discussion on one track.

They can have what's called a leadership team—the leader, the blackboard member, the recorder, and the observer—which has been at work as the meeting progressed. Andrew Mack, for instance, has been taking charge of the blackboard in this session. He's been writing down all the important contributions, so any member who is tempted to investigate a side issue has only to look at the board to be pulled back. When the talk gets going so fast that people forget the blackboard is even there, the leader can remind them, or Andrew can himself. So can Hortense Nelson, the recorder.

In her job she is doing somewhat the same thing Andrew is doing at the board. But she's not going to erase it. She is making notes of the gist of the discussion so that she can write up the main points to mail to the members before the next meeting.

Joe Ellison, the one who talks so well and has so quick a grasp of problems that he used to scare the others into silence—what's he doing? Joe has a new role, and although his job keeps him from saying anything, he doesn't mind. He's the observer, who makes notes, not on the discussion, but on how the group discusses. Since the observer usually doesn't talk until the end of the meeting, we'll leave him, for the time being.

The back-and-forth of argument, the hammering away at a problem, goes through several stages until decision seems almost to come of itself—of which more later. When these decisions do come, they are better decisions and will be more effectively carried out than those obtained by voting. It is implicit in the very act of voting that some members disagree and perhaps will stay forever unconvinced. "If they'd only listened to me, this wouldn't have happened. . . ." In the traditional meeting members are very likely not to "listen to me." In this kind it is imperative that they do.

About forty minutes before closing time the leader breaks off the discussion and gets the group to round it up. Then the members decide what problem they want to work on at the next meeting, volunteer for the various leadership jobs for that meeting, and are ready to make out what is commonly called, for obvious reasons, their p.m.r. sheet—post-meeting reaction sheet.

On this they write what they thought of the meeting. What was good about it? What was only fair, or worse? Were they able to say the important things they wanted to say? And so on. (See samples, Appendix I.)

Filling out these sheets is their first backward glance at how the meeting—as a meeting—went. Joe Ellison can start them on another.

For this is Joe's moment, and for what is left of the time he becomes in effect the leader of a new phase of the meeting. From the highlights of his notes (which he had time to go over while the group made out their p.m.r. sheets) he asks questions to start the group on what is known as the evaluation—when they look back on the meeting and the participation in it. Reminded by Joe's questions and the specific details he has to give them, they can talk it all over and analyze it.

This is the part of the meeting which, surprisingly enough, is hard to bring to an end. Everyone likes reconstructing the past—of a meeting as well as a football game. "If we'd done this . . ." "If somebody had only given John a chance there to come in with his point . . ." "If we'd stuck to the subject, instead of . . ." "Well, next time we'll see that . . ."

But come to an end it does, and with it the meeting—preferably two but not more than three hours after it began.

4. CAN THE CHAIRMAN STOP BEING BOSS?

Before any chairman decides to take on this kind of meeting, we suggest that he figure out first whether he can stop being boss. For that flattering role of expert and authority will be his no longer.

Take Edward Norcross, for instance. He's a fine chairman: hard-working, good-humored, quick, and a "good executive." He already has more jobs on his hands than anyone else in the community. "If you can get Ed Norcross," people always say, "everything will be all right." So they get Ed Norcross, or perhaps Mrs. Norcross, who runs as many committees as he does.

Almost all members, beginning with the chairman, bring to a committee their old ideas of how a group should function. Even more important, they bring old habits of group action. Past experience has convinced them that any group is only as effective as its chairman, no more and no less. The successful chairman, in all the groups they've met with so far, has been a combination of spark plug, organizer, and driver. Using his own powers of persuasion, he can be relied on to bring together the people who, he feels, will be the most likely to carry out his plans.

Those plans are already well thought out. He comes to the first meeting with an agenda. He explains to the members what the

That old and established relationship

problem is, how they are going to tackle it, what they should get done. He hands each a carbon copy of his agenda and then, with that completely likable smile of his, he sits back and says, "All right. Let's go."

He has not once pounded his gavel. In fact, he hasn't any visible one, but it's there all right, and the members know it. They follow his lead—faithfully or supinely. If they aren't happy in the situation, they drop out rather than question his authority. They expect authority in their chairman. Frequently they have been chairmen themselves, exerting that same kind of authority. In fact, their sole yardstick for measuring a group's performance is how quickly and effectively the chairman gets them to carry out his program. This is what his committee expects of Ed now.

So it's a major hurdle for both Ed and his members to get over that old and established relationship between them—much more of a one for Ed. The members will usually change their ideas without much difficulty; sometimes just one good demonstration creates enough enthusiasm to do that. But changing their basic habits is another thing. It is bound to be slow and arduous, for it is learned through doing. At first the members will devise various kinds of resistance—and so will Ed.

He can't get over this hurdle unless he feels a real, not an assumed, conviction that his members are capable of solving their problems—not his interpretation of the problems but theirs. He may think he's convinced, but when it comes right down to it— well, isn't he really better prepared to understand what it's all about? Could he really trust the members to figure out the best solutions? If he were being completely honest with himself, he might even ask: What if they agree on something I don't like?

He can bolster his confidence in his members if he considers three points, the findings of investigations* made since the 1920's.

1. Though a few superior individuals may be better in their judgment ability, the average of group judgment is superior to most individual judgments. When a problem involves a

---

* Some of these are: G. B. Watson, "Do Groups Think More Efficiently Than Individuals?" *Journal of Abnormal and Social Psychology* (1928), pp. 328–36; T. W. Thie, "Testing the Efficiency of the Group Method," *The English Journal* (1925), pp. 134–37; K. Gordon, "Group Judgments in the Field of Lifted Weights," *Journal of Experimental Psychology* (1924), pp. 398–400; M. E. Shaw, "A Comparison of Individuals and Small Groups in the Rational Solution of Complex Problems," printed in *Readings in Social Psychology* (1947), edited by Newcomb and Hartley; N. R. F. Maier, "The Quality of Group Decisions as Influenced by the Discussion Leader," *Human Relations*, Vol. III, No. 2, June 1950.

number of people, group thinking will produce better results than the thinking of any one person.

2. A group is more likely to accept good suggestions than to reject them.

3. Groups do not err as soon as the average individual does.

A chairman should also remember that the reward for waiving his old rights and privileges includes the greater interest with which the members will carry out decisions. For when he steps down as authority and lets the members really share the responsibility of planning, defining, and deciding, he is bound to enlist and release a new energy in his group.

This approach to groups and committees won't help a chairman to drive harder and faster toward his goal. It doesn't provide ways to make him, the leader, feel or become more important. It does help make the group more productive and drives the members harder toward their own goal.

If you are a chairman can you see yourself fitting into that framework? Can you change your committee habits? Can you agree with the following premises? That members of your committee bring to it all, or almost all, of the knowledge, experience, and ability needed to enable it to get what or where it wants; that members are responsible individuals who, with proper stimulation and assistance, are more capable of finding working solutions than you alone; that the group can achieve its purpose, without your control, if you can create and maintain a situation in which the members will usually be willing and eager to contribute.

If you can agree with these premises, can you rebuild your habits around them?

Lao-tse, the Chinese philosopher, once put the problem very neatly into one sentence:

> Of a good leader,
> When his task is finished, his goal achieved,
> They will say,
> "We did this ourselves."

How to Go About It

The tool with which the leader works, in order to stimulate talk and contributions from all members, is the question. This is not used in the way to which he may be accustomed, the traditional technique

post-meeting reaction sheets, and, most valuable of all, the members' self-evaluation.

Some Pitfalls the Leader Can Expect to Meet

His biggest problem at first is the feeling of loss of control of the meeting. Without the use of his old habits and techniques, he may find himself swinging to the other extreme and letting the meeting run without any guidance for fear of doing something wrong. He can avoid this quandary quite simply by not trying to reach perfection in one jump. For the first meeting, if he selects and uses a few fun-

Don't interrupt unless it's important

damental guides and ignores the others, he will come out surprisingly well. Every leader has to decide for himself what his key guides should be. These may help:

1. Plan the opening questions in advance.
2. Don't lecture or answer—ask; ask the group as a whole.
3. Don't interrupt unless it's important.
4. Watch for chances, when the group seems to have talked out a point, to push toward the goal.
5. Relax: it's the members' responsibility too.

The natural impulse of any leader new at this game is to direct questions at individuals. He falls into this trap in response to those moments of silence to which we referred before. Such moments throw the leader who is a novice into a kind of panic. He feels that they are lasting to embarrassing lengths and he must somehow, anyhow, bring them to an end. Or he yields to that impulse out of mistaken kindness. Seeing one or two members sitting there saying nothing, he feels he must provide them the opportunity to speak.

What happens when he does direct a question to an individual? Usually he catches that person off-guard. The unhappy member flounders and takes one of three courses: a) simply talking at random while he tries to pull his thoughts together, b) coming up with some face-saving answer that has little or nothing to do with the previous discussion, or c) blurting out whatever comes to mind and retreating into sheepish silence for the rest of the meeting. (There is the rare group member who sees what is happening and—when addressed by name—is skilled enough to give an answer leading back to the point under discussion before the silence fell. The leader had better not count on finding such a paragon in his group!)

The upshot of questions directed to individuals is that the leader has taken control away from the members and is firmly back in the saddle, with a tight grip on the reins. The member-centered meeting has reverted to the chairman-centered type. One way for the leader to check this impulse is to remind himself frequently that he is there to help, not direct. Another is to remember that if a few members don't talk, that is of minor importance for the present. They will later unless he startles them into retreat with questions directed to them.

If the meeting really gets out of hand the leader can use questions directed to individuals to regain control but, unless the group has a few members who resent his control and fight it, he will not have a member-centered meeting thereafter until he resumes the stimulating approach which invokes it.

Another possible difficulty in an early meeting is the sudden realization that the main discussion part of the meeting is almost over and no solution has been reached. If this happens the leader can say something along the line of, "We have just so many more minutes before we have to stop. Let's see what we can pull together out of what we have up there on the board and what we've been saying here. What have we agreed on so far?" He will normally be both pleased and astonished at what the group will then produce.

Problem behavior—with which all chairmen struggle—is a pitfall in itself. In these meetings the leader shares this problem with the group. It is one of his real compensations for giving up his authority. Since this is a group problem, not primarily the chairman's, it is discussed in later chapters.

Behind this kind of leadership behavior lie a number of research findings. They show that there are a number of leadership functions and responsibilities which are performed best if the leader shares them with the other members, others he can only perform himself. The ones to be shared are:

1. Creating and maintaining a permissive atmosphere, so everyone feels free to talk.
2. Setting the group's goals.
3. Getting real consideration for all points of view.
4. Keeping the discussion on the beam toward solution of the problem being explored.
5. Summarizing the discussion when it has gotten confused, out of hand, into a stalemate, or has just produced too much too fast.
6. Exploring the group's activities to find ways to improve them.

Believe it or not, this leaves the leader with quite a lot of functions and responsibilities that he does *not* share. First of all, he is the group's stimulator and guide. Everything he does is done to ease the group's job of setting its goals and reaching them. He makes sure that members understand the area in which the group has authority to act or to reach a decision. Although he is careful not to interfere with the content of a discussion, he controls, with member consent, the way the discussion proceeds, maintains order in it, and suggests or gives the nod to uses of different techniques. He is the key to development of good morale and teamwork, he leads the others in facilitating the solution of member frustrations or conflicts, and he obtains guidance and support from a higher authority, if needed.

He also has some less obvious responsibilities. In some groups these have to do with the members themselves: raising their level of motivation, increasing their readiness to accept change, and furthering their individual development. In all groups he tries to help

the members achieve a high quality of decisions and, when pertinent, of action to carry them out.

5. THREE TO GET READY

If the leader is thinking seriously about changing his role from boss
to stimulator, he will want to know about the help that he can have
from the other members of a leadership team. Not a once-over-
lightly but details. How much of the load can they carry? How do
their jobs help the group produce more? What should their attitude
be? What do they have to learn? Specifically, what do they do?

The Blackboard or Easel* Member

Let's go back to that possible meeting where the members are
sitting in a semicircle with a blackboard making the closing of the
U. Andrew Mack, the once silent Mr. Mack, is standing there writing
the meeting's problem across the top of the board, and all the others
are watching him. He is there, not by reason of his silence, but because he volunteered to do this job at the last meeting. To tell the
truth, he's enjoying it.

Whatever he puts on that blackboard should be important, and
it's up to him to recognize importance when he hears it. When the
members start digging at the problem, they'll ask themselves, "What
is the situation right now? What are the main facts?" And as they
mention those facts, he will put them down. In no time he'll have a
good-sized list—long enough to make the members take time to look
it over, to think about the items, and wonder which ones they have
missed. After a few seconds George Costello will come up with an
additional one; so will Virginia Fox. Then there will be a silence.
Someone, perhaps the leader, will say, "Well, is that it? Is there anything else important?" Another pause while everyone thinks. The

---

* If the facilities do not include a blackboard, an easel can be substituted. A pad
of blank newsprint paper can be clipped to it. As each sheet becomes filled it
can be torn off and fastened to the wall with masking tape or clipped to a wire
strung where all can see it.

leader breaks it by saying, "If that does it, how about trying a new statement of the problem? Who'll try it?"

At that point Don Seaman suddenly comes to life. "Wait a minute, we've forgotten something. It's important too. How about . . . ?"

So Andrew picks up his piece of chalk to put down Don's fact, but someone else interrupts with, "No, that isn't right; it's this way . . ." In the discussion that follows, Andrew gets the wording on the board the way the group wants it, and they all move on to the next phase of the discussion, the obstacles or objections.

What has the blackboard done to the discussion?

For one thing, it has kept the members' attention focused. For another, it has put their ideas where they can see them, where they can study them to decide which points are missing. Also, it has probably kept them from bringing up the same point several times. They all have the same facts, the agreed-upon facts, right there where they can see them, where they can't help but see them, and refer to them.

That is how the blackboard works.

But what about Andrew, trying to write what the group wants him to write? After all, he's just an ordinary, fallible group member. How can he do it? How can he learn to recognize key points when he hears them and get them down fast enough to keep up with the discussion?

Surprisingly enough, it's not as difficult as it sounds. Some people will be better at it than others, of course, just as some people are always better in certain jobs than others. But almost any person who is intensely interested in helping the group produce can do it. The core of the technique is this: the blackboard member concentrates —completely concentrates—on the thread of the discussion, as a tennis player watches the ball. If he's listening intently enough he forgets to be self-conscious. He forgets to worry over how his performance looks, or whether he's choosing the right words, or what the members are thinking of him. He doesn't have time, in fact; and out of that intent listening the vital points seem to come to the surface and identify themselves.

Once he has recognized a key statement in the discussion, he can either write it down immediately, without asking for confirmation, or break in and ask, "Shall I put that point down this way?" Which he does depends somewhat on the temperament of the chalker. It also depends on the stage and tempo of the discussion.

Say that the group is at an early stage, breaking down a subject into its elements, as when listing obstacles. Everyone is trying to analyze that subject, to figure out what problems in it need to be resolved. Members may be thoughtful, on the whole quiet. When a member speaks he does so tentatively, and he usually makes an easily recognizable point. Or points from members may come fast in a kind of pell-mell fashion. This requires quick work on Andrew's part—but he can do it if he writes the gist of what he hears without bothering to ask for phraseology.

Similarly, he may have to write fast when the group is trying to reach a decision. For when a solution is just around the discussion corner, vital points may come very suddenly indeed. And these are not worded as separate points. In the thick of concentrating on the solution, an idea which pleases everybody may just burst from one member; then ideas start popping from all sides, and all Andrew can do is get down key words. He does not interrupt then if he can possibly avoid it. If he does he distracts, postpones, and generally messes up the discussion, which may have been almost at a decisive point.

If he's been concentrating, Andrew is well aware of what's happening. He recognizes the approaching crisis in the discussion even more than the members who are involved. His ear is tuned for just that. As soon as the going slows down a little he breaks in to ask, "Have I got everything? Have I said it right?" If he doesn't do this, the group may soon find that what he has written has lost all meaning for them—and along with it a valuable part of the discussion.

His being in a position to do this actually provides him with a tool of considerable power. From his strategic spot at the board, he can help—or hinder. If he's concentrating hard enough on the discussion, he's temporarily like the coach of a football team; he can see which players are doing well today, what plays could be most successful; he can see when the team is slowing down, when it's stalled, when players aren't pulling together well enough. He can see when a change in attack would help the team along—and he can provide it.

For example, by asking someone, "Did you mean . . . ?" he forces both the member and the group to decide whether that point is worth putting down. That may start a discussion over the point and its wording. "Is that good or bad at this moment?" He has to decide.

He may cause useless backtracking, or he may sharpen the issue to make a decision come sooner. He may bring things to a complete halt, or redirect them into a more fruitful channel.

It's not at all impossible for the blackboard member to take entire command of the situation by directing questions and writing down only those points which contribute to his personal objective. It has been done, and not to the speedier reaching of group ends, either. For when he takes advantage of his dominating spot in this way he becomes a boss, an autocratic leader, and restricts the group by his own limitations.

It is not likely that Andrew's ego will goad him into taking over the show. But in case it does (maybe he's always had a hidden yearning to be boss), the members will soon be aware of it and resent it. If some of them become obviously annoyed, or the production of the meeting is threatened, someone may suggest an evaluation then and there. If things aren't too bad it is better to wait and let the observer bring the question up when he starts the evaluation at the end of the meeting. It then falls in with the general looking-back-at-their-own-performance of the group and doesn't make Andrew a single target.

The Observer

It was no great coup to get Andrew Mack working well at the blackboard, but it was tougher for Joe Ellison to make himself a good observer. For until the last twenty minutes of the meeting (unless the group wants an evaluation earlier) Joe has to be quiet, and it's not easy for him. He has dominated more meetings than most people have ever thought of attending; he's a natural at handling words and ideas and, most of all, people.

He did the job of observer a few meetings ago, but it could hardly have been termed a success. He gave in to that hardest temptation of all: he broke into the discussion several times. At the end he was supposed to start evaluation on the part of the members, to spark it. But Joe being Joe, the job was too much for him. When he was finally given his chance to raise the questions the meeting made seem most important, he took over and talked for the entire twenty minutes. But tonight's meeting is his second go at it. He is controlling his propensity to talk, and he is concentrating on the others' performance. He is not only learning how to handle the job; he is developing a new slant on how members, himself included, act in a productive group.

So he sits with the group in the semicircle, but he says nothing. He makes notes frequently, glancing first at this one, then at that. He notes how often Hortense Nelson speaks, how often Mrs. Buck; whether another member feels free to talk, or starts to and gets stopped because someone else is louder and more emphatic. He sees whether one or two members monopolize the conversation, and he's watching the leader too—how he affects the group and how the group affects him.

Although he is not concerned with subject matter as such, he follows the discussion enough to note when members go off the subject, when they backtrack or quibble. Or, if the members leave the job of keeping the discussion on the subject up to the leader and don't bother to do it themselves, he notes that. He's been called, and rightly, the eyes of the group. He is their ears as well, listening for pertinence, frequency, and interaction of the contributions.

He becomes—and even Joe Ellison can manage to do it—a kind of alter ego for the leader, who is necessarily absorbed in the progress of the discussion. No matter how hard he tries, that leader gets too caught up with the "what" to be fully aware of the "how." Some of it, of course, the leader senses and realizes, just as do some of the members. There was that point in the discussion when, down the table to his left, one whole segment of the group was quiet for too long, but he didn't have time to stop to get the situation right. Or that other time when he let himself get into a debate with the member on his right. He didn't mean to, but it happened before he realized what he was doing.

Joe Ellison, in his job as observer, is there to do the remembering and the realizing for him. And for all the others members as well.

The Evaluation

Unless the group has asked for his observations earlier, the end of the meeting is Joe's first chance to talk. While the others are writing down whether they thought it was a good or bad meeting and why (on the post-meeting reaction sheet) he works over his notes. (See examples in Appendix I.)

Then the moment finally comes when he is practically the leader of a second, though brief, meeting. Like the leader, he does not try to run that meeting; he tries to stimulate the members to run it. But he has to start it off, to spark it, using those notes and observations he has been making as the opening signal. Like the leader, he asks questions on the general aspects of what he's observed, the highlights, and then gets down to asking questions about specifics. They might run about like this:

"I wondered, early in the meeting, whether everyone really got the same idea about the objective. That time when J. B. said . . ." (referring to his notes) ". . . and a little later Hal commented that . . . I wondered whether they were both saying the same thing in different ways or whether they really meant different things. The group seemed to support J. B.'s version. Had you overlooked a problem at the start to cause that confusion? Did nobody really understand it? Is that why you came back to it later?"

Or, if the discussion clearly went off the subject: "You spent about ten minutes talking about . . . Did that really have anything to do with the subject? Why do you think you went off in that direction? How did you finally pull out of it? Could one member have pulled you out sooner?"

If much of the meeting was bad he might lead to a basic weakness by asking, "Well, what goal have we been trying to reach tonight?" If agreement comes soon, "Have we succeeded?" If not, "Why not?" If they did, "How did we make it?" "What were the turning points?"

(Many observers use "we" instead of "you" to lessen any feeling of criticism.)

By this time, if not much sooner, the members should be well launched on an analysis of one phase or another of the meeting and their activities in it. They are like bridge players who delight in going back over their hands to discuss how they played them. Joe is the official kibitzer on the play of forces within the group, but, unlike the usual kibitzer, he is provided with notes to start that backward look. That is what he is there for. His questions may be helpful in themselves, but they exist as a springboard for the group to reach their own conclusions.

His questions focus the thinking of the members on what the group did well and what it might have done differently, perhaps better. They are objective, impersonal questions about decisive points in the discussion: "Would we have made more progress if we had . . ." (taken a different course or dug more deeply into the problem). It's as though he had taken an X-ray of the group's activities and reproduced the highlights and shadows.

He may have been asked to watch for specific types of participation (see Chapter 13) and restrict his notes to jotting down evidences of those. He may focus on how well the members stay on the subject. He may watch particularly how they support one another in drawing out facts or developing viewpoints. Or he may concentrate on the leader's performance (at his request), noting where he could well have cut in, or given support, or asked questions which would have furthered the discussion.

Can Joe do all this? Yes, strangely enough, Joe, or Andrew Mack, or even Mrs. Buck can do it. (Although Mrs. Buck will have to conquer her tendency to be superconscientious; she will want to begin at the beginning of her notes and read them through, a sure way to put people to sleep and waste evaluation time.) Like the job of blackboard member, the observer's requires concentration of a selective sort. Andrew, at the blackboard, listens for one kind of thing; Joe listens for another.

The first member to take the job of observer in a group often finds it difficult though absorbing. If he feels he wants to practice it first, he can observe one meeting without starting the evaluation at the end. Instead, he and the leader can go over his observations later in an evaluation session of their own. This tryout is usually enough to enable him to do the whole job at the next meeting.

Normally he doesn't start the group's self-evaluation until the end of the meeting but he may break in any time it seems important with, "Do you mind if I ask a question?" If the leader or one of the members feels that things are bogging down badly, that contributions are too uneven or even acrimonious, the group can ask the observer for help. His questions, judiciously asked, can usually get the conflicting forces in the group back into balance.

The Recorder

There is one other semi-silent member of the leadership team, the recorder, who makes a record of the highlights of the meeting, the gist of the discussion (not the details, which no one remembers or cares to remember). In addition, like a secretary, he lists the members present, the place, the names of the leadership team, the time and subject of the next meeting. He prepares a report which, if they wish, is sent to the members before the next meeting. This report is not read at the meeting as minutes would be.

Like the blackboard members, the recorder has to do a tall job of concentrating. Perhaps he can best help himself to do that concentrating by jotting down, "Subject," "Content" across his page (see sample, Appendix I). He may not fill his page in that precise pattern, but it makes a useful start. He too can focus the discussion, or bring it to a halt, by asking for the repetition of a point "to be sure I get it into the record correctly." But to push the discussion one way or the other or to join in it is not his function. He does so only in extreme cases, when no one else rallies to help a badly confused group.

During the evaluation he often has to struggle between his own itch to get into the talk—often the most alive and intense of the whole meeting—and his need to get the highlights on the record. He wants to say what he thinks about the meeting, and if he does, you can count the record lost from then on! And not well lost either, for the evaluation is one of the most valuable parts of the session and needs to get into the record.

The leader, in introducing member-centered meetings, and the group in subsequent sessions, can use the leadership team or parts of it whenever and however desired. At the beginning, use of the team is usually very good. It reduces the leader's traditional stature and at the same time can give him good support, as discussed in the next chapter. It brings several members into the new method immediately and it emphasizes the differences among leadership functions.

Later, when the group has learned to work successfully, the members may feel that the full leadership team is unnecessary or that it is too rigid and interferes with progress. They may decide that the leader can handle the blackboard without dominating the meeting. They may agree that an observer is no longer necessary—that they can start evaluation from post-meeting reaction sheets, or even without them. There is no reason for them to continue these separate roles when they are no longer needed. Either or both can be abandoned. They can always be started again, either as a one-shot booster or continuously if the group later feels the need.

6. IT'S NEW TO THE MEMBERS, TOO

The members of most groups have attended regulation meetings until they know the old line-up by heart. Some of them are ready for anything that promises a change. They don't see that they have anything to lose and they might just stand to gain. They are curious and willing. Others are open-minded but not dissatisfied enough to want to accept new responsibility. Without some preparation, the first meeting could be a spectacular failure, after which even the willing members might be ready to return to the comfortable familiarity of *Robert's Rules*. The preparations take a little time, but they are worth it.

The Problem Census

Since members of a member-centered group are going to share responsibility for its accomplishments, they should begin that sharing even before the first meeting. Ahead of time, then, the leader should find out what they think the group's job is going to be. He has a clear idea of the goal, but he does not know what the others think. It's probably pretty hazy to some of them, and even if they have defined it in their own minds, the chances are slim that their thoughts correspond with his. A common understanding of basic purpose is the first thing the group needs to achieve. Therefore by telephone if possible, or by letter if necessary, he lets the members know as much as he does about the essentials of the job ahead and asks them to be thinking about what the reason for the group's existence is, what its problems are likely to be, and how the group might go about solving those problems.

This preliminary query has several purposes. In the first place it alerts the members that they are going to have to consider problems and help make decisions which were formerly left to the chairman. Second, it starts their minds in the direction of deciding the group's goal. Even if they give it very little conscious thought, they will be more ready at the first meeting to reach the necessary common understanding.

Third, their answers—if they come up with any at this preliminary stage—give the leader a rough idea of what they are thinking. This may be at complete variance from what he was thinking. Often it is, and so much the better for him to find it out at once.

Fourth, on the basis of whatever response or reaction he receives, the leader can decide whether the members are ready to try all the attitudes and techniques of these member-centered methods at once, or need to have them introduced gradually. Using a piecemeal approach, a leader helps the members learn to handle the different responsibilities a few at a time. In an all-at-once introduction, he explains the whole idea to the group and then starts right in with a full leadership team and group evaluation. The rest of this chapter outlines an introduction of each type and suggests what the content of the discussion should be at this first meeting.

The All-at-Once Introduction

Experience has shown that the best way to handle this is to have a preliminary talk with the key members, followed by a dress rehearsal with the leadership team.

The Preliminary Talk

The need for the leader to have a preliminary talk with the other three key members is of course obvious. The general idea, even if already discussed with them, is not enough. Now he wants them to form the group's first leadership team. In preparation for the first meeting the talk needs to be specific and practical. It also helps for the leadership team members to tell the others that the leader is planning a different way of handling meetings.

The Dress Rehearsal

This is a must for the leadership team if the first meeting, coming up in a week or so, is to be a success. The members of this all-important team need both a common understanding of their jobs and a chance to practice them. The four of them can best get the feel of what they are going to do by having a preview session, which isn't for keeps and where fumbles won't make any difference. The rehearsal can do double duty by having the subject of discussion "Leadership team jobs and how to handle them."

The leader directs the dress rehearsal, using the questioning technique. While he discusses with the recorder and the blackboard member, they make notes as they will at the first meeting. The observer stays out of the talk. When the session is over and the post-meeting reaction sheets filled out, he practices his technique by raising questions about the leader's performance and that of the other two members. All four then evaluate the joint performance.

The rehearsal comes to a close with two final bits of arranging. One is the selection of a subject for the group to discuss at its upcoming meeting, and since the first job for any group is to be sure the members have a common understanding of what they hope to achieve, a discussion of the group's purpose is the logical choice.

The other necessary bit of preparation is for the leader and the observer to arrange that the first questions to be asked at the end of the meeting will be aimed at the leader's behavior. Discussing his actions objectively will set the pattern. It will also confirm what the leader has been saying about not being an authority and about being ready to accept criticism.

The Meeting Itself

Word has been sent out before this meeting takes place that it will vary from the usual. But there can be as many misconceptions about what is going to happen as there are members. They need a quick explanation from the leader of the key points of leader activity and member participation, and how these are geared to helping a group be more productive. The plan is to hold member-centered meetings for enough sessions so that all can become familiar with the innovation. If, after a fair trial, the members would prefer the more traditional procedures, the group can revert to them.

But the explanations are not over. The participants need to hear from the other members of the leadership team. Each, in fact, should give a *brief* summary of what he is going to do in the meeting and why.

The meeting then begins, focusing on reaching a mutual understanding of the group's purpose. It closes forty minutes ahead of time so the members can fill out their post-meeting reaction sheets, and the observer can raise his questions to start an evaluation of the meeting by the members themselves. He starts, as agreed, with the leader's performance. "Do you think," he may ask, throwing the questions to all the members, "that X was a bit too dominating at such and such a point? Did he give you enough chance to talk? Why didn't somebody break in? Were you all satisfied with the decision?"

Or, if the leader kept too much in the background, the observer may ask, "Did X have some special reason for not helping more when everybody was trying to figure out . . . ? Should he have suggested alternate approaches?" Just a few questions along one of these lines should be enough to start the members on their own backward glance at the meeting's strong and weak points, and at how well they worked together as a group.

Finally, although the members will probably suggest that the same team and the same leader carry on, it is only sensible for the leader to do so. Until the group learns to work together smoothly, it needs the same person as leader.

But it is important to have different members assume the rest of the team jobs at the next meeting. It shows the group that the new method does not belong exclusively to the original few. It reinforces what has been explained and demonstrated: that every member is an equal participant. In later meetings teams can serve for two consecutive meetings so they can benefit from the first experience, but not before each member has performed at least one leadership job.

The Piecemeal Introduction

Few groups are ready to tackle all of the new method at once. They are interested, but certain aspects seem strange and questionable to them. The blackboard may seem a first-rate idea; they may like the recorder, too. But they may be dubious about the other ideas. This is approximately the reaction any leader can expect when he suggests a change in their meeting habits to members. If it seems wise to progress through the familiar to the unknown, their comments can reveal a workable, step-by-step schedule.

The changeover might be still more gradual. It is possible for the leader to make many of the changes without even mentioning that his methods are different. His first step is to change his own technique into that of not answering questions but turning them back to the group. Though he is definitely in control of the meeting, the members feel a greater sense of freedom. Without knowing why, they are more inclined to talk. At the same meeting the leader can man the blackboard himself and ask the usual secretary to get down the gist of the discussion rather than to make exact minutes. At this meeting, too, a common understanding of the group's purpose is the basis for discussion and here as well the members agree that the subject for the next meeting should be considerations of the problems which will have to be solved in reaching that goal.

From then on how fast the leader moves depends on the receptiveness of the group. The post-meeting reaction sheet, confined to two questions, is probably the next step: What did you particularly like about this meeting? What did you particularly dislike? Although the members do not sign their names, they may make their comments hesitatingly. But once they realize that the leader really wants their opinions, they will give them more freely and honestly as the meetings go on and they begin to think about themselves as a group. Further evaluation then seems not only reasonable but usually happens of itself. Without knowing it, they have paved the way for the observer. From then on a leadership team seems a natural and useful tool in the struggle to get more from meetings.

The face-saving factor for all concerned in either of these introductions, or any modification of them, is that the whole group is inexperienced. The members realize that they are all in this new effort together. They want to make their meetings more productive and the ways are at hand for them to use. When one or another member bungles, as he works to convert these attitudes and techniques into habits, it is part of the common effort, and no one is likely to hold it against him.

7. KNOW WHERE YOU'RE GOING

Almost everyone works better when he knows not only what a job is about but has some part in helping to make decisions in it. What should by now be a truism has been tested by several studies in recent years. One of the most rigorous tests was conducted by an industrial psychologist who found that groups of factory workers having instructions carefully explained to them did not significantly increase their output. Those who had both an explanation and a chance to make some of the decisions relating to how they would act on the instructions did significantly increase their output.*

At meetings, as well as in work situations, too few people get a chance to help make decisions. The usual chairman has been asked, or told, to take the job. Matching zeal to a sense of duty, he works out an agenda, perhaps a year's schedule, and goes off to his first meeting, content that in due course he will get his group's active support.

Due course doesn't always follow. His group is like any other; it is made up of human beings who balk at being expected to carry out a program which they have had no part in shaping. On the surface they are compliant and receptive. Underneath—whether they acknowledge it or not—they are still balking. They resent doing special jobs for the group. They fail to come to meetings or they come late. They fail to contribute when they are there and they give the problem only partial attention, feeling subconsciously that after all it isn't their problem—it's the chairman's.

What's more, that problem is probably seen differently by each member. The chairman has thought it all out; he explains it at the first meeting and then goes on to Heading No. 1 on his agenda, taking it for granted that he has covered the situation. He has, but only for himself. The members jump to their own conclusions and interpret his explanation accordingly.

Remember the Railroaded Meeting described in Chapter 2? The group met five times, each time going ahead with plans and arrangements very much in the manner of the famous knight who leaped on his horse and rode off rapidly in all directions. This was a "training committee" on whose shoulders fell the job of planning a year's program for hundreds of people. It was at the fifth meeting that one of the members was defeated in an argument. Irritated and hurt, she sat back in her chair and said suddenly, "Well, then, I guess I just don't know what we're here for!"

She honestly didn't know. Neither did the rest of the committee really know. At long last they went back to what should have been

---

* See "Level of Knowledge of Requirements as a Motivation Factor in Work Situations," by Tomislav Tomekovič, *Human Relations,* Vol. 15, #3, August 1962, Tavistock Institute, London.

their first consideration: they got down to discussing what kind of training they should offer.

No group will really know or be able to be creative unless its members figure out for themselves, at the start, preferably at the first meeting. The leader of our projected group stimulated the members to do some preliminary thinking about its purpose with his telephone calls or letters. And so they may have done. Yet the ideas of each are likely to take off from the point that seems of greatest importance to him, and travel a different road from that of the others. Those varying roads must converge as rapidly as possible, or some of the group's energy will be dissipated.

Reaching a Mutual Understanding

If the leader does not have an agenda in his hand, what can he substitute? How is he going to start this first meeting? How can he get a roomful of people, even if there are only fifteen of them, to agree on a definition of their purpose?

He starts the meeting with several questions to which he has given considerable thought ahead of time. He has some notion of what the members think to be their mutual purpose—culled from the responses he got to his telephone calls. He bases his questions on these. If he feels the need for others, here are some which may prove useful. Through answering these, the leader and the members can circle the field to come down for a pinpoint landing.

Why is there a need for this group?

What is the immediate situation in respect to that need?

Why are we interested in it?

What do we think we can do about it?

What is a reasonable goal for us to aim at?

And with certain groups he might ask:

For whom are we planning? What will be their reaction? Is there any way we can include their thinking in our planning?

For whose benefit do we want to achieve our goal? What are the advantages of achieving it for us? For them?

The leader asks these or similar questions, and when the answers come he questions those answers. He questions a statement he thinks may not be clear, or one that sounds obscure; he questions whether every angle has been brought up, always throwing these questions to the group as a whole, not to an individual.

Throwing questions to the group

In the process of this general investigation, the group has not only come up with an agreed definition of its purpose, but is charting its course. The members are planning their project, shaping their own agenda, and as they do so they come to have a more personal sense of possession about the job on which they have embarked. At the end of the meeting they should be ready to say, with finality: This is what we think we can get done and this is how we hope to go about it.

While this has been going on the blackboard member has been writing down one point after another. All that is said cannot of course stay on that board; there isn't room. So what he does is list facts pertinent to one stage of the discussion. When the group has moved on to another he erases with safety because the recorder has a list, too, and can read it at any time.

Both blackboard member and recorder will inevitably find that the discussion has not limited itself to defining the group's goal. They should be prepared for this. Any number of problems that will have to be solved will occur to the members as they think about what they hope to achieve. As these are mentioned they should be listed, at one side of the board, and held in reserve. It is unlikely that the group will have time to set priorities among the problems at this first meeting. But that haphazard list of them can form a starting point for the next meeting, when the group begins to come to grips with its problems and what the members think they can do about them.

III: PRODUCTIVE METHODS

8. STEPS IN PROBLEM SOLVING

Any group that comes together to get a job done is going to have to
spend a good part of its time solving problems. Whatever the level
or composition of the group—members of a standing committee of a
national association, community workers, people from a section or
division or on the board of directors of a huge organization—the
group is only meeting in the first place to pool its thinking on the
solution of problems.

How good the decisions they reach will be depends, of course, on
the caliber of the people making them. It will also depend on their
freedom to explore the problems and possible solutions from both
their own viewpoints and those of the persons affected. If the chairman uses his authority to force or manipulate them to accept his
solution, or the one he and a few others have settled on previously,
the meeting becomes nothing but a formality. His solution may be
the best, but nobody can be sure of that until all the members have
worked their way through to it, with full consideration of all its
implications.

The Pattern

When the basic components of a problem-solving discussion are
extracted, they can be put together into a recognizable pattern,
which will emerge something like the outline below. The chart is
included as a device we hope may help members keep track of
where they are in their discussion, and may provide some brake on
their natural impulse to wander off into irrelevancies, generalities,
anecdotes, and personal opinions. The detailed, play-by-play account
of each succeeding stage may prove a brake, in turn, on the im-

pulse of either the chairman or a dominant member to push things through.

| AGREED GOAL
 └ PROBLEMS EN ROUTE
    └ SELECTING THE PRIORITY PROBLEM
       └ THE PRIORITY PROBLEM
          | Agreed definition
          Related facts
          Obstacles to solving
             └ POSSIBLE SOLUTIONS
                | Pros and cons
                Possible results
                   └ RECOMMENDED SOLUTION
                     | ACTION PLAN

The main headings can be put on the blackboard, to one side, or tacked to the wall on easel paper so that the steps will remain in sight.

Listing the Problems

After a commonly understood goal has been set, the members aim their next discussion at bringing out the problems that they will have to solve before that goal can be reached.

The leader starts with questions and continues to use them as a means of producing the free discussion and the flow of ideas he —and the members—are after. "What do you see as our problems? Our difficulties?" In a community group he may well ask, "What's our opposition? Is it apathy? Strong, entrenched feeling? Lack of understanding?" In a standing committee, "Is the problem one of communication? Of money?" And in a large organization, "What will be the bottlenecks? Will that department be willing to change?"

The leader may well feel he's inviting the flood with his questions. He may be. But if that flood is relatively on the subject of the major problems, he lets it come. The first points may be obvious, some later ones minor, and others merely gripes. They are listed on the board anyway, as rapidly as possible. Even the griper's problems should be listed, since the sooner he has them off his chest, the sooner he will be able to concentrate on the discussion. Occasionally there is even a clue to a valid difficulty in what he is saying.

Sometimes the opposite happens and total silence greets these questions the leader has so carefully thought out. If that silence is not broken for good by the first reply, the leader can profitably divide the members into buzz groups, assigning to each the task of listing the problems it sees or foresees.*

During the stage of listing the problems on the board, the quibbler or the tidy-minded one among the members will be tempted to view some new problem being brought up as part of another and suggest the two be combined. Or someone will be eager to point out that a certain "problem" is really a "related fact"—a category which appears later on the chart. If the group lets itself fall into this trap of weighing niceties, it will only succeed in wasting time and diverting energy. The object now is simply to list all the problems the members can anticipate, at full speed.

If the group starts wandering off the subject, there are the life lines of a member-centered meeting to be thrown out. The blackboard member or the recorder, both of whom are trying to put down only pertinent data, can break in with, "This is all very interesting but I'm not getting any real problems to put down." Or the members themselves can put a stop to this waste or monopolizing of time by calling for a summary.

Should the listing stop for lack of some essential piece of information, there is nothing to do but recognize the situation as soon as possible and let one member volunteer to produce it at the next meeting or, if necessary, call in an expert.**

Selecting the Priority Problem

When the listing seems finished and after the leader's "Well, let's take a look at what we have. Anything more that should be there?" it's time to move on to what the Army calls an "estimate of the situation." Which of the problems, listed so rapidly and with no attempt at placing them in any reasonable order, should be taken up first? Because of its importance? Because its solution will speed the solution of others? Because of some deadline?

* See Chapter 9.
** See Chapter 14.

Solving the Priority Problem

After finding out whether they all see and understand the chosen problem in the same way, the members list the facts relating to it. These should be facts they are powerless to change: the existing laws, for example; some regulation; a matter of physical distance; a customary routine which would take more time to change than the group has at its disposal. Some of these may already have gone on the board in that cursory listing of problems, recognizable now for what they are.

The major chore ahead is a fresh listing on the blackboard, perhaps flanking that of Related Facts. This highlights the obstacles that will have to be faced before a working solution to that priority problem can be found. These obstacles may appear with no difficulty or require buzz sessions (Chapter 9) or role-playing (Chapter 11) to get produced. Once they are listed, the group subjects each one to some analytical questions: Is it fundamental or superficial? Is it only a symptom of more basic trouble? If so, what is that basic trouble?

Then comes what is sometimes a final listing: possible solutions. This is the result of such questions as, "What are we going to do about these basic troubles?" And, "What *can* we do about them?"

The possibilities listed often include solutions tried by other groups faced with similar obstacles. In rare cases one of these will provide a clue applicable to this one. The more usual situation is that the group hopefully dredges up what it remembers and, after some thought, lets it go. No alternative remains but to start the thinking and listing process again. The blackboard member erases the previous lists (the recorder has their duplicates) and the chore begins.

Here, if the group wishes, it can use the process known as "brainstorming," introduced early in the 1950's by Alex Osborne.* It is based on the theory that one man's brainstorm can spark another man's solution.

Every possible solution the members can think of—good, bad, irrelevant, out of line—all are mentioned and listed without pausing for criticism or afterthoughts. This type of unblocked, pell-mell expression of ideas, important when the problems went on the board, is equally important in this technique.

Finally, these come to an end and the weeding-out time follows.

---

* *Applied Imagination* (New York: Scribners, 1953).

Some of the proposals can be discarded at once: they certainly *were* out of line. Others look fairly acceptable but collapse when subjected to the pros and cons of how they would actually work. ("That would cost too much; people would refuse;" "top management will never buy *that* one;" or "won't the members in Texas or Ohio resent that?")

The Before-Decision Stage

In the early stages of a discussion the attitudes of the members toward the issue are often unknown or unexpressed. As the discussion goes on most of these positions become known. The members either state them or ask questions which are clues to their attitudes. The facts and forces underlying these positions also become apparent. Each group member is then able to make a kind of mental separation of his fellow members' positions into those there is some chance of changing and those about which little can be done at the moment. Gradually a comparatively limited area in which there is a chance of agreement emerges.

When this has happened the leader or a group member can summarize the discussion to that point, to clear the air and restore a sense of order. Unless it is premature—forcing the members to commit themselves before they are ready to do so—a summary can help. It can provide a base for a fresh start and may narrow the field of disagreement. If the conflict seems a difficult one to resolve the leader can ask A—on the side opposed to a solution—to restate B's point favoring the solution, in his own words but in a way acceptable to side B. And vice versa. This process requires each side to think through and gain at least partial understanding of the other's attitude.* It also can end a disagreement, by showing that the opposing sides are in reality giving a different interpretation to the same facts.

Role-playing (see Chapter 11) can also be used when the conflict seems an emotional one, or one based on the imponderables of human behavior in a projected situation.

When one or a few members hold out strongly and stubbornly against some aspect of a solution which has gained the approval of the others, it may be well to pause and backtrack. This seemingly unchangeable stand must be respected rather than pushed aside.

---

* See Wendell Johnson, "The Fateful Process of Mr. A Talking to Mr. B," *Harvard Business Review,* Vol. XXXI, #1, January-February, 1953.

The members holding it may see or sense a difficulty which hasn't occurred to the majority. Or their opposition may come from a personal feeling: perhaps their arguments did not get the attention they felt they deserved; perhaps they did not have a chance at full expression earlier. ("If you'd only let me finish what I was trying to say. . . .") For the others to urge the minority to go back over the ground, analyzing the points as they are raised, may be enough to remove the sense of grievance. Or either side may see matters in a different light as they do this analytical backtracking.

Reaching a Decision

What the members at this type of meeting are after is an agreement on a decision—specifically, here, on a creative solution. It is not the comparatively simple matter of voting. "When you go to a meeting and know you are going to vote on a point," commented one member after a session of a member-centered type, "you have your mind pretty well made up ahead of time. When you go knowing that the decision must be reached by agreement, you go with a mind at least partially open. There's a big difference."

Sometimes a decision based on a suggestion pointing a new avenue of thought will come very quickly. It suddenly seems right to all the members, and so it may be. But without subjecting it to the testing routine of considering the pros and cons, or of role-playing, it may produce a kind of unhappy double take.

More common is the truly "integrated solution," the decision reached by agreement. The members piece together the constructive elements of their positions in a way all can accept. The process is not a compromise. It is rather like putting together one jigsaw puzzle from a box which holds parts for three or more puzzles. The member putting it forward may have thought it out consciously or unconsciously. It respects the taboos of the members and so can be worked out within the tacitly accepted area of discussion.

The group's next step is planning to put the solution into effect, and if measuring results is important this is the time to provide means for doing it.

Acting on the Solution

In carrying out the action, the discussion group can serve best by acting as a review board, delegating responsibility for the job to one person and appraising progress until it is finished. Its remaining function then is to determine what further steps, if any, it may wish to take.

9. BUZZ GROUPS IN SMALL MEETINGS

In the late 1940's, Dr. J. Donald Phillips, then head of adult education at Michigan State College, developed a device called "Phillips 66" to enable the audience at a large meeting to have a share in what was going on. He called it "66" because he instructed the audience to divide into groups of six and gave each group six minutes to come up with a specific question for the speaker of the meeting to answer.

Since then his original technique has been used and adapted and its application varied until it is now a familiar standby for large and small groups. It is no longer called "Phillips 66" but is known as dividing into "buzz groups" or "buzz sessions." The noise made by the small groups comes through as a general buzz; someone so labeled them and the name stuck. This device of divide and produce is best known for its use in large meetings, but it is also a particularly effective way to help small groups focus on a problem.

Why Buzz Groups Work

Among the reasons for the high productivity of the little groups are the following:

1. Each person has more chance to speak than in a larger group.
2. In the intimacy and anonymity of a small, face-to-face group the members feel freer to speak than in a large group.
3. Small groups talking together in close quarters in the same room exert a pressure on each other to arrive promptly at good results.
4. Several small groups can cover more ground than a larger one in the same time.
5. Finally—let's face it—not only in large meetings but even in

the best member-centered ones some of those present may lose interest for a time or simply tire of sitting in the same chair in the same position. Breaking up into buzz groups changes the pace and has a generally enhancing effect on the members.

Uses of Buzz Groups in Small Meetings

In writing of a small meeting here we are thinking primarily of a group of not more than about fifteen members, usually concerned with solving a problem of mutual interest. In such a meeting, buzz groups are useful for a wide range of purposes. When general discussion isn't bringing all the necessary information, well-chosen assignments to buzz groups can produce more. When members are too tense or too timid to express themselves, or if they don't know where to begin, buzz groups do away with their reluctance to perform before an audience. In a group that has not yet learned to control its dominating members, buzz groups can free the suppressed ones for a time (and develop their ability to resist domination afterward).

When conflicting views or interests are causing trouble, buzz groups of members holding one view can be put to work examining the other members' side of the question, or the leader can assign one or two buzz groups to list all the pros of a suggested solution, the others to list the cons. If several solutions are being considered, one buzz group can examine each to gauge its probable results and the reactions to it of the people who would have to carry it out or would be affected by it.

The one purpose we have found for which buzz groups are not good is asking several groups to recommend a solution for the same problem. Each group may become enamored of its own solution, making the finding of common ground more difficult. It is better, when the decision-making stage of a discussion is reached (see page 50), to have every member exposed to the positions and points of view of all the other members.

When to Use Buzz Groups

The leader (or indeed any member) can suggest the use of buzz groups whenever he thinks they would be useful (even if the leader only feels he has to do *something* to change the atmosphere). The task or tasks assigned will, of course, relate to the difficulty under discussion. If the real problem at the moment is member tenseness or domination, the buzzing can serve the dual purpose of relieving the situation and at the same time exploring a subject. "What's the priority problem to be solved?" "What ways are there to reduce this obstacle?" "What will be the impact of this section of the law (or the meaning of this directive)?" "Who are the key people in the community (or the organization) whom we could approach to help make this change?"

How to Use Buzz Groups

The leader asks the group to break into clusters of three to six, depending on its size. He can do this by chance: "Will the five of you in that corner form one group?" or "Will you count off by fours and all the ones form a group, all the twos form another, and so on?" Or he can plan their composition for a purpose, as suggested above.

The members pull their chairs into tight clusters and he gives them their tasks, with the shortest time limit appropriate to the complexity of the tasks and the size of the groups—anywhere from five minutes to twenty, with a half-hour as the outside limit. If the tasks are too complicated for a half-hour he'd better break them down further. These tight deadlines not only save time but tend to keep the buzzing focused on pertinent points.

He then tells them what ground they are to cover and what kind of result he expects them to produce within the allotted time. He does not appoint leaders because doing so would obstruct the groups' fluidity and freedom. He does, however, ask each group to select a reporter before it begins its discussion.

After the Buzzing

The leader, observing and listening to the buzz groups until the allotted time expires, decides whether to stick precisely to the stated limit or to extend it briefly because the tenor and intensity of the discussion indicate that a few minutes more might be highly productive.

When he does stop the buzzing he has each group report all its points at one time if the groups were assigned different problems. If they were assigned the same problem interest can be kept high by having each group report its most important point, then making as many rounds as necessary to get all points on the blackboard.

With all points on the board the next stage is general discussion of each point, in any order the group wishes. A showing of hands as to how many members wish to discuss the first point first, the second point first, etc., is usually a quick and satisfactory way to establish a priority list. The group may find that some points need more intensive study and decide that buzz groups would again be useful.

Buzz groups, in short, can be used to stimulate thinking, provide short cuts to solutions, or simply operate as a device for enabling the whole group to gain information or ideas more swiftly or more completely.

10. BUZZ GROUPS IN LARGE MEETINGS

Our definition of a large meeting, as opposed to a conference, is this: it is limited to one session and is held in one room.

Also, by our definition, a varying proportion of the time spent in most large meetings is wasted. In chairs constructed with a T-square in mind, the people in the audience have to sit still whether they like it or not. The air is bad. From the platform come words which they cannot refute and, as the words go on, some of them spend the never-ending minutes trying to keep the lids from closing entirely over their eyes. They may be able to get in a question at the end, but even this single exercise of their mental muscles is usually denied them. Someone else is always quicker to get to his feet or wave his hand. In no time the chairman is saying, "I'm afraid we have time for just one more question."

Still, people go to these meetings, sit through them passively—or in a state of angry frustration because they cannot voice their disagreement—and by the next day have forgotten all about them. Their habits and ideas remain, for the most part, unchanged by what they have heard.

What can be done to make large meetings both creative and productive?

The solution lies in giving the audience an active part in what is going on. It makes no real difference whether the session has been called to persuade or to provide instruction; its impact will be far greater when the audience shares in the events. The way to help them do so is to break a large meeting into little meetings, into buzz groups or some variation of them.

The only factor really limiting the use of buzz groups here is one of time rather than of numbers. Given a meeting lasting as long as three hours, as many as 250 or 300 people can express themselves through the small groups. The responses or ideas they produce can be sorted and grouped during the interval between the first and second halves of the session. But when the entire meeting will last less than two hours, buzz groups are not practical for an audience of more than one hundred—at the most.

For the Question Period after a Lecture

The first time we saw this method used, perhaps a hundred people sat facing the stage of the auditorium. There was a lecture first, and then the chairman counted off the people sitting in odd-numbered rows into sets of three. He next asked each set to turn around, face the three immediately behind, and with them make up a group which was to have six minutes to decide what question it would most like to ask the speaker.

Six minutes is a very short time in which to reach agreement; on that first occasion it seemed an impossible assignment. But the very fact that the time was limited sped production. (Since the early days of their use, buzz groups are now often given a somewhat longer period. But there must be a limit.) The urgency was such that those small knots of people all over the room worked with such concentration that they were unaware of the other groups.

Time was called. The slips of paper with their questions were collected and passed up to the platform for the speaker to answer, working his way from the top of the pile down. The people in the room turned around and again faced the stage, but they were no longer a passive audience. They had a stake in the action going on. No one knew which question would come first, and the sense of possession which all human beings feel about something they have helped to create took over. And the questions themselves were far better than those of the usual meeting, which often inquire about a point the speaker has already elaborated, or are used by a member to air his own knowledge or particular grievance. Apparently when six people have to agree on a question, someone among them will spot the meaningless one. They have a group pride in making their question worth asking, and it usually is.

Buzz Groups are simple to use. The essentials are:

1. Before the meeting, explain to the speaker or panel members what the method is. Allow ample time for questions to be dealt with.
2. Explain the method briefly to the audience before the question period begins.
3. Count off two rows as a sample, to show them how to proceed.

Basing a Lecture on Questions

A lecturer with a good knowledge of his subject and plenty of courage can make a talk particularly rewarding if he is willing to base it on buzz group questions and plan it on the spot. He begins by saying something like:

"You all know what my general topic is—but tonight, instead of my trying to guess what you'd like to hear about it, I'd like you to tell me." When the buzz groups have handed in the questions he quickly appraises them and makes his talk around the principal requests. His presentation may have little similarity to the content and order it would have had if he had prepared it in advance, but he will have a more alert and responsive audience.

As a Stimulant

Recently we used buzz groups to stimulate the thinking of about thirty-five high-level officials of a multilevel organization who were reputed to be more inclined to enjoy their authority than to use it well. The question put to them was "What difficulties do you have in getting your orders carried out effectively?" It proved to be a subject the officials concentrated on with gusto, and thirty minutes later the twenty-eight difficulties they produced were on the blackboard. They chose seven as being most important and for the rest of the meeting each of seven buzz groups analyzed one difficulty for reasons and solutions. In a follow-up meeting the next week, they pooled and refined their findings. Thus in a very short time the experience and knowledge of the group were focused and made the basis for exploratory activity.

For Information and Comment

Buzz groups have been used at the opening meeting of a large PTA to elicit from the parents and teachers present their preferences as to the programs for the suceeding year. The PTA also uses them in the opening sessions of conferences to learn from members the accomplishments they hope for from the conference; or the topics they feel of paramount importance to discuss in small groups; or in any large meeting when the effort is to engage the thinking and gain the participation of those present.

Listening Teams

An audience can be involved and put to work even before the question period at the end of a lecture. It can be formed into listening teams, a suggestion for which we are indebted to Dr. Leland Bradford, Director of the National Training Laboratories of the National Education Association.

Before the lecture begins, the chairman of the evening divides the audience into sections, each of which is to be responsible for listening to what the speaker says with a different question in mind. Here are four questions, for four sections, which he suggests: Which of the speaker's ideas won't work for our community (or our organization)? What further ideas for attacking our problem do the speaker's statements suggest? What are the barriers we must reduce to carry out his suggestions successfully? What are the next steps we should take?

After the lecture, each team breaks into small buzz sections to discover the reactions of the members and report the important ones to the audience as a whole. (Obviously any number of questions and teams can be used according to your needs.)

An audience can also be divided into teams for watching as well as for listening, so that each section concentrates on a specific problem or question. The entire audience sees the same documentary film or role-playing scene. Each section is instructed to follow through one angle and report on it. How can that angle be adapted to their group's needs? What is useful for its purposes? What would work for its problems? When the scene playing before their eyes comes to an end, each team divides into small buzz groups which then come up with the various questions or problems.

There are, in fact, endless variations on the theme of buzz sessions. Vary the device as you please and as you need, remembering that for at least the portion of the large meeting in which it is used you have automatically eliminated boredom in the audience.

11. ROLE-PLAYING

Role-playing is a valuable technique for solving problems creatively. It is acting out a situation to inform, persuade, or create a deeper understanding in the group involved. The members themselves play the parts, occasionally with a rehearsal and a few props, more often using only their imaginations to direct them. For several years role-playing has been proving itself a surprisingly useful device to make a situation come alive for both the actors and those watching.

It makes an ideal springboard for any meeting, but its use extends to many other situations. At any time it can help members of a committee to anticipate how they, or those whom they are trying to portray, might feel in that situation. It can be used as a short cut through tedious explanations of facts; it can serve to illuminate and throw new light on a problem in discussion. It can test a future situation, or, even before discussion on a problem has begun, it can give a graphic picture of what that problem will be. In short, there are endless ways to adapt it to the problems of any group.

Why It Works

Role-playing is based on an old truth we have taken a long time to rediscover: if we are really to learn anything, we need to learn it from the inside out. We have to start at the emotional center. If the imagination is captured, the emotions are involved as well, and the result is that Mr. X, for instance, actually feels as Mr. Y might feel. Mr. X has been told often enough, but just telling didn't do any more good than just telling usually does. If X takes the part of Y and tries to put himself in Y's size 10 and rather worn shoes, he begins to get a surprisingly new slant on a problem. And the audience shares that new feeling.

The basis of it all is that we love a play (or a novel) in which we can lose our own identity and become the hero or heroine. Even a bad play will find us biting our lips, sitting on the edge of our chairs, and so living through the situation being played before our eyes that we cry, or laugh, or ache to get up there on the stage and take over.

Curiously enough, the same magic works even when nothing whatsoever has been paid for seats. For example, we sat in the audience with perhaps forty young graduate students who were studying social service when role-playing was used as a training device. One of their members came on a mock stage to interview a pathetic elderly woman (actually another social worker) who was trying to get advice about what she should do when she was released from a sanitarium. It took over a half-hour for the young student to figure out a practical solution, and during that time the audience grew more and more tense. When at last she came up with a workable idea, the audience gave an audible sigh of relief and broke into applause.

How It Began

The idea of acting out a situation is probably as old as the first cave man who dramatized the time he killed an outsize lion. Or as new as the latest parent who says to his child, "Now, this is what you do when you are introduced to someone: just put out your hand— no, no, your right one, not your left. This is your right hand . . ."

But the credit for applying it to a totally different kind of situation belongs to a psychiatrist, J. L. Moreno. Back in the 1920's in Vienna he tried the technique (in a form which he called psychodrama) as a means of helping his patients back to mental health. The sociologists and educators who got a good look at his method in action when he came to this country decided that it could be adapted to everyday problems.

Since then, the core of the method Moreno developed has been applied to an increasing number of situations and has seldom failed to clarify them. During World War II the Office of Strategic Services used the technique, among the other tests psychologists worked out, to judge applicants for particularly dangerous work. OSS found that how applicants looked and what they wrote on paper were not enough; these failed to give a clue to the real man. What was needed was a way to discover not only a man's breaking point, but whether he was a leader or follower, how he would act in situations demanding tact, quick thinking, or forcefulness; whether he could take a hard blow, not only physically but socially. Truths such as these, deep and often hidden, are hard to come by. In less than a week, using "situation tests" in which the candidate had to play certain roles, the examiners were able to decide whom to accept or reject. Subsequent performance of those chosen proved the virtue of the methods.

The Army uses role-playing, which it calls "exercises," "hypothetical situations," or "reaction testing." Vocational guidance centers use it to anticipate future problems; factories and businesses to improve employer-employee relations; teachers to help make clear a subject; theological seminaries to prepare students for situations they will face with their future parishioners; and, as we have seen, schools use it to train graduate students. There are many other instances, but the important point here is to show how it may be used for meetings, small or large.

How You Can Use Role-Playing

There are two kinds of role-playing: the prearranged skit, and the one that evolves, spontaneously and naturally, out of the course of a discussion and has not been arranged in advance. Either is helpful in solving the particular problem for which it is geared.

The prearranged skit is a valuable short cut. It can be used to brief an audience on information the members need to have, and to dramatize a situation which they will later analyze and discuss. It presents a situation so much more vividly and appealingly than could a speech that it fixes that situation in the audience's mind. It's there. What's more, the participants remember it and build on it. What is still more, those watching the skit share in it emotionally. Consequently they leave the meeting far more ready to carry out the group's purposes. Besides conveying information with a real impact, role-playing can create understanding and produce a higher percentage of resultant action. In any money-raising campaign or, indeed, in any meeting whose purpose is action and persuasion, it is a superb technique.

For example, a group that was working to persuade citizens to vote for the county-management form of government sponsored a meeting. All who were there, perhaps fifty or more people, had been asked to function as a kind of speakers' bureau: to talk later to citizens' associations and groups of all kinds. Most of them were willing to help, but were unprepared and uncertain.

After a few points of order the chairman explained that several on the committee were going to put on a skit representing the kind of situation that would face the members of the audience when, later, they went out to address meetings. The actors would try to demonstrate first the type of speeches to be given, then the reactions and questions which were likely to follow.

Around a table at the front of the room, the committee began the skit with explanatory speeches from two members. Then the others asked questions. For example: "You said that a county manager could save this county X dollars. Now, I'd like to know where you got those figures." And, "How do we know we'll get a good county manager? Why won't he just be a political appointee?"

And so on, one belligerent, another pleasant, another a heckler, and still another the typical apple polisher, without whom no meeting is complete and who often can make an audience turn around and go in an opposite direction.

"Wel-l-l now," said the actor, clearly relishing his part, "I just want to say I think maybe we're being a little hasty here tonight." He took off his glasses, polished them slowly, and smiled out over the audience. "I think we may be being a little unfair to those fine men who've been taking care of our county here now for a good many years. Maybe they could have done a better job; I won't say they couldn't. But they're just folks like the rest of us, and like this manager you're talking about putting in. I've lived around these parts for longer than I'd care to say, and we've been getting along all right. Our children have had a mighty fine education, better than most of us had, I dare say. . . ." And so on.

At some point the questions being put on the mock stage shifted into free-for-all questioning from the audience, and by the time the meeting broke up, everyone there had had a better briefing in county government, pro and con, than hours of explanatory speeches could have done.

This kind of skit, like any type of role-playing, needs little pre-arranging. In no sense is it putting on a real play with rehearsals, props, and written lines.

Actually the role-played situation, even of this prearranged kind, has most spontaneity and reality if little more than the situation and the various characters the actors will play are decided on before the meeting. In the county-management skit, for instance, one character had to know that he would be the typical fact-finder, another the type who insists on knowing what would happen if . . . , and the third, of course, that he should clothe his opposition in the guise of a seasoned, genial mediator.

Too much coaching or rehearsing is likely to deaden the performance. Meet once, figure out what the core of the problem is and what you want to get across to the audience. Then decide which characters will best dramatize that problem or issue, try a quick test run to get the feel of it, and let it go at that.

If you explain to the audience at the meeting that this is an almost spontaneous affair, they will like it the more on that account. And you can almost always count on the player's imagination to persuade him to do his best in the role, once it is given him.

So, use the prearranged skit to convey information; to present a situation for later analysis; to involve a group of people in a project and stir them to greater conviction and action.*

Spontaneous Role-Playing

This kind of role-playing (sometimes called reality-testing or sociodrama) is like the prearranged skit in that the players share others' feelings and the members of the audience share some of its results. But it differs in purpose in that it happens on the spot; it

---

* For example, role-playing was used to explain and convince a PTA meeting of about seven hundred people that the schools needed better sex education. First, a scene was enacted in which questions on sex were badly handled. Second, a scene showed the wise handling of the questions through the schools. Next was a scene involving a large number of actors who discussed the problem at a simulated PTA meeting. Last, a film was shown which, in the sense that the audience became imaginatively involved in the course of its story, had some of the effect of role-playing in itself. A point specifically mentioned as a successful by-product of the role-playing was that a great many people necessarily had to act in the scene which portrayed a PTA meeting. Acting the parts in itself served to persuade the participants.

is not prearranged or prerehearsed. It grows out of the occurrence within the group of some kind of situation that can be better understood if it is acted out.

Even the freest discussion cannot bring out every angle of a problem. Even farsighted committee members cannot always anticipate how other people are going to feel as a result of a committee decision. The most productive group runs into difficulties; one member feels his arguments unfairly ignored; another consistently fails to make any contribution. Or a group may feel almost certain that it is deciding rightly, but there may be a lingering doubt in the minds of some, if not all.

In any of these situations, and in others, the group can make giant strides toward solving the problem by letting a few members volunteer to act it out. The term "reality-testing" means just that. They are testing how people feel, or would feel, by pretending they are those people faced with that situation. Curiously, they may find, as they imagine themselves in the part, that they are feeling differently from what they had expected. As X found his emotions different when he thought himself into Y's shoes, so do both the group members acting and those watching.

Role-playing is a way to explore the emotions of others; by semi-experiencing a situation, the actors are able to perceive and feel it more completely. They can draw a much deeper and more valid understanding of what factors may be involved in the problem. Since the reality they are testing is not the eventual reality, and the parts they are playing are not for keeps, they feel a real willingness to play them—once they have been introduced to the technique. But more of this later.

Here is a listing of the various uses of this kind of role-playing, resulting from moments at which some member, or several, of a group could well say, "Let's role-play it," or, "Let's role-play it at the next meeting and find out."*

1. For testing ahead of time how a group decision might result.
2. To prepare to meet a future situation.
3. To let some disagreeing or irritated group member get his grievance off his chest (and understood, as well).

---

* We are indebted for the itemizing of these instances to a clinic group at the 1948 National Training Laboratory in Group Development, Bethel, Maine.

4. To get a better understanding of the point of view of others.
5. To develop special skills on the part of a group member or to develop understanding of group situations.
6. To present various courses of action (for decision).

Prepare to meet a future situation

But since role-playing as a method of solving problems is so unfamiliar to most group members, a listing of the occasions for its use is perhaps not enough. It is not possible in so short a book to give examples for every one in that list; but specific instances may be suggestive enough to persuade a leader or group member to ask: Could we solve this problem by role-playing? Would role-playing be a way out of our impasse? Would we be on surer ground if we role-played the effect of our decision?

To Test Emotional Response

A workshop was held to study relationships between pupils and teachers. Toward the end of the session the delegates felt that they had reached conclusions which would improve the teaching habits at their various schools. But how were they going to go back home and justify those changes to their fellow faculty members? How were they going to persuade them to make the change? Would their colleagues listen to the reports with open minds? Or would they resent those enthusiastic recommendations?

Someone said, "Why don't we role-play? Why doesn't Miss Garnsay," who had brought up the question of how the reports would be received, "play herself, addressing her own faculty, and see how it comes out?"

Miss Garnsay played herself without any hesitation. She thought it would be easy. Several others played the faculty, who were being "told."

The faculty met. They conducted usual business. Then Miss Garnsay got up and said, "I think you will all be interested in hearing about the recent workshop, the decisions we reached, and the new systems we think all of you will want to use here as a result."

She went happily into her speech, but the "faculty" was not happy. As she gave them the facts, they found they definitely resented her attitude. Why should she assume they would like to turn the whole system upside down just because she had gone to a workshop? To her astonishment (and, when they got around to thinking about it later, to theirs), the members of the group who were playing the faculty were angry.

"You didn't even ask us if we wanted to hear your report. . . ."

"You just walk in here and upset the whole handling of my classes without any understanding of what my problems are. . . ."

"What you say may be all very well for some high schools, but it will never work in mine. I would rather resign than try to . . ."

Needless to say, the group then started to figure out an acceptable way of presenting the decisions of the workshop to their local faculties, knowing the results of the several-day session would be almost wasted unless they could interest, involve, and persuade the teachers at home to carry out what the few had learned. They role-played several methods until they found one that had positive rather than negative results.

To Test the Response to a Decision

A group of foremen in a factory used role-playing to help them out of a particularly difficult situation with the men under them. It was necessary that the men wear safety devices which they hated and found excuses to avoid. How could the foremen present the problem in a convincing way? How could they anticipate the men's attitude enough to be convincing? Role-playing gave the answer.

In another instance, a committee planning training for groups of volunteer workers reached, on paper and through discussion, what it considered a good decision. It involved a lengthy annual report that they wished those volunteer leaders to fill out. Would they do it?

"As I look back on being such a leader," one member put in, "I can say that I think the thought of another report would infuriate me. You people haven't the faintest idea how much work goes into that job anyway—not only work, but money and gasoline and telephone bills and all the rest. Those leaders haven't time, I tell you. They won't take it."

"No," said another, "I think they will appreciate it. After all, it's for their own good. They'll be forced to look back over what they've done. It will help them to see their own mistakes."

"Nobody ever likes anything that's for his own good. . . ."

They role-played it and were convinced that the ex-leader was right. They not only changed the report form, but in a very short time set it up in a way that would enable the leaders to supply the needed answers and facts quite simply.

This last episode is typical of the use of role-playing not only to test future response to a decision, but to test the decision itself. Or, more properly, as a way out of those deadlocks that may occur in a group discussion when neither side can accept the other's viewpoint. To test which decision would be right, role-play it both ways. Is your feeling, your response, better when this happens, or when it is done that way?

Helping in a Group Problem

A large conference was held on welfare problems. In one of the small groups meeting to work on a section of the large issue, there was one member who tried, again and again, to get her points across. Each time she failed to persuade the others, who turned their attention to the words of a more dominating member.

At last she grew angry and burst into the talk with, "I feel I'm being discriminated against in this group. I've been treated unfairly since the beginning of our meetings. If this conference is to work on our problems, I'd like this to be a problem. I'd like you to take the way you're discriminating against me as a problem!"

Suddenly aware, for the first time, of how she felt, they did take her feeling as a problem; they role-played the preceding discussion with the two key figures playing each other. As a result, the play of personal forces in the whole group shifted. The role-playing in this instance accomplished three things: it let the frustrated member realize the dominator had meant nothing personal; it gave the too dominating member a new insight into what she was doing; it gave the whole group a feeling of drawing together, of patience, sympathy, and understanding. They became a more cohesive whole as a consequence.

When to Role-Play

Groups which are used to role-playing come to recognize, almost automatically, those moments when its use is indicated; others learn very soon by trying it. If a problem, a decision, a situation touches or will touch the feelings and emotions of people, role-playing will provide a better answer than discussion. How can you judge this, however, the first time?

Again we use the core of suggestions worked out by the National Training Laboratory clinic group.

1. The scene should reveal or deal with a valid problem in human relations.
2. The problem should be clear, single, and specific; it should never include related problems.
3. It should be one the group is capable of acting out; i.e., one in which the players can understand how the characters might feel.
4. It must mean something not only to the people who are doing the role-playing, but to the people who are watching it. It should, if possible, mean approximately the same thing to all of them.

Let us add that it is most often effective when the problem to be played involves only a few people in any one scene. Human problems usually focus on a very few individuals and the fewer the players the easier it is to follow promising trends and recognize significant findings.

How to Go About Role-Playing

Introducing Role-Playing

A leader experienced in directing spontaneous role-playing can sometimes introduce it successfully to a new group without preparation or even giving it a name. At a critical point in the discussion he may simply say, for example: "This is a tough problem. If we could get some clues as to how the people we are talking about would feel about this proposal, we might find it a lot easier. Would two of you be willing to act out what might happen when two of them hear about our proposal? Who'll be Mrs. X? And who Mr. Y?"

But such an informal approach is risky for a leader who has not yet acquired polished skill and flexibility.

There is bound to be a certain resistance on the part of one or several members to a device that is completely unfamiliar. Until they try it, they may think it childish, or feel self-conscious at the thought of playing a part. These and other reactions can be anticipated. Tackled head-on, they are only strengthened, so take it slowly. At some meeting, when its possible use is not likely, it can be described as a technique the group may eventually find helpful. If possible, a few members (primed ahead of time) may play out something simple and objective that can in no way disturb anyone present.

Warm-up Session

On the first occasion when role-playing seems the solution to a problem, a special warm-up session (the playing out of a fairly meaningless episode) may help to melt the self-consciousness of the group. But on succeeding occasions the warm-up need be no more than the necessary discussion of the situation—where it is, what the occasion is, what kind of person each character is.

After a group has learned to use role-playing, trying a preliminary episode is not only unnecessary but may even be harmful. For when a group is deeply involved in thrashing out a problem, a warm-up scene may take the edge off playing the real one. Role-playing should be a striking-while-the-iron-is-hot proposition to achieve what it's after.

Setting It Up

Props: Clear one end of a room, shove the table around and push away the blackboard, place needed chairs, and give one actor something to read if his part indicates that. But don't go any farther. The more fuss, the less spontaneous the whole scene will be.

Casting the characters: At this point, the leader needs to be sensitive to the strengths and weaknesses of the people within the group. Asking for volunteers is the best, but even the volunteers may, that first time, miscast themselves. It is vitally important that no too vulnerable member—the timid one, the easily hurt one, the inarticulate one, etc.—be allowed to play a part in which those sore spots in his personality will be revealed for all to see. Nor should anyone who already feels unpopular with the group, rightly or wrongly, be allowed to play someone unpopular. Cast the characters that first time—indeed, the first few times—in such a way that someone whose importance and liking are unquestioned in the group will play the unappealing role.

For the other roles it is well to let people play familiar parts the first time, parts which are so automatic as to be almost second nature. Then, as the group repeats the same scene immediately after, as they usually want to do, have different members take the roles. Later, when used to role-playing, people are much better able to assume parts quite opposite to themselves.

Similarly, as a group grows accustomed to the device (and to one another), members can choose to play those parts which they feel will help them the most. In fact, once the original shyness wears off, resistance does too, and people are able to play any number of parts they never expected they could.

Character Descriptions: Obviously X would get very little good out of playing Y unless he had some notion ahead of time of what Mr. Y is like. For example, here are clues given to several men who put on a role-playing demonstration in the Army:

. . . a very conscientious man who is scared to death of doing anything irregular.

. . . man who hates his superior and whose superior hates him. His transfer papers are in so he doesn't feel any need to pull his punches.

. . . man who loves to pitch headlong into large production problems. Happiest when involved in the hurly-burly of getting out a lot of work. Home situation is unhappy and he likes to put in overtime.

The actors must have a mental picture ahead of time, even though it is only the briefest sketch. Very little is needed to remind them of people they know who share those characteristics. They try to think how those people would feel and act. From then on the imagination is quite competent to take over on its own.

Involving the audience: If role-playing a situation follows directly on discussion and argument about that situation, the members of the audience seldom need to be told to identify themselves with the characters. Indeed, they often feel so strongly about their own angle on this problem that they cease being objective. Like the audience at a high-school baseball game, they care only about their team; the other team is the enemy and its plays (or points of view) are discounted or ignored. This state of enthusiastic participation, or identification, though exciting, hardly makes for sympathy with another viewpoint.

Hence a word to those who are going to watch role-playing is good. Ask them, if they are violently opposed, to try to place themselves in the part of their opponent in the argument. Use the put-yourself-in-his-place technique. Try to get them to spread their sense of identification beyond those playing their point of view, or they will get no emotional understanding and be no nearer a solution when the role-playing is finished.

Another device to involve the audience is to ask one or two to watch for specific reactions or ideas. Or ask the group to sort out the various angles of the problem and agree to watch for revealing behavior in relation to them. What do they think (making notes at the time, if they like) of what A feels? Is it warranted? Is it the way any of them might feel? How would they feel if they were A, or B, or C? Why are A and B and C behaving the way they are, anyway? Why are they, the audience, feeling as they do while they watch? If a solution seems to emerge inevitably from playing out the situation, is it really inevitable? Does it seem the right one, at last?

The best means of involving individual members of the audience is to get them quickly into the actual playing of roles. One method is to change the participants each time a situation is replayed, but the leader must weigh this advantage against the need of the present players to take different roles. Another method grows out of the process. When the playing of one scene brings out the need for another, additional people play the new roles.

A further method is multiple-role playing, in which several pairs or groups play the same role simultaneously and then join in a common analysis of the various experiences and results. (See page 73.)

Cutting It Off: It takes a considerable measure of experience to know just when to cut off the action, to realize that the high point has been reached and what would follow would be on the downgrade, both in content and feeling. Most novices at role-playing let it go on too long. It is an effective device regardless, but it is more so if it is cut at the peak, when either the solution or the emotional profiles are sharply defined. There is little help we can give on

Knowing when to cut off the action

this, since the skill of knowing when to end—in a book, or play, or when the guests linger at the front door—is never easily come by.

The best advice we can give is this: keep aware of the specific purpose of this particular bit of role-playing. Cut it off as soon as it either provides the information, skill, or understanding the group is after or seems sure not to provide it.

Evaluate and Play It Again: Once the scene has been cut off the leader may lead an analysis aimed at enabling the group to gauge the significance of what happened, or he may postpone the analysis until the scene has been replayed either by the same persons in different roles or by different members.

If the purpose is to gauge the resistance to a proposal without going into the emotions involved, having the scene played another time or two by different members is a logical next step. The leader then breaks the group into buzz groups with the job of listing the reasons given in all the plays for resisting the proposal. Once on the blackboard, each of these points is available for appraisal, analysis, and the planning of counteraction.

If the purpose of the role-play extends to helping the group understand the feelings of the persons involved, the leader usually leads an analysis at the end of each scene. He may ask the players how they felt as they were acting their parts and then turn the question to the audience. Needless to say, this immediate talking-it-over session is essential to clinching the reactions experienced and solving the problem which occasioned the role-playing.

How did the members who took part feel when such and such a thing happened, or was said? Were all the members satisfied with the action they just watched? Would they have interpreted the character or point differently from the way A did? Do they feel B picked up all the important points? Was there an obvious angle overlooked? What would happen if that angle had been picked up and the players had carried on from there? Did a completely new problem arise out of playing that scene?

These, or any number of other questions, may emerge, and the best way to answer them is to play the scene again with the roles exchanged or with different members playing them. From the various actions and responses to the roles, the group can test its convictions or arrive at new ones. Obscure forces and factors become clear, and, in a measure, all experience the situation and are able to understand it more completely.

This use of role-playing is, in a small way, the same kind of thing the armed forces do in a large way when they have a war game. They create a hypothetical situation in which two armies or fleets are to fight in certain areas. Some factors are stated and others are left unknown. At the planned moment the two forces begin acting out the problem. Observers watch at strategic points to see what techniques and stratagems are used and how successful they are, and decide what others might be more so.

Pitfalls: Role-playing can be absorbing. It is usually far more fun and more engrossing than just sitting in a chair and discussing.

The obvious but important warning, then, is that it should not be used just for the sake of ending boredom, or to show off a new trick; its use should be restricted to problems or situations that warrant it.

Nor should it ever be used in an instance when it will play upon a really serious emotional illness on the part of a member. Illness of that sort is in a psychiatrist's bailiwick, not in a discussion group's. It's up to the leader to recognize this, whether role-playing is new to him or not, and steer away from deep-seated difficulties. Once the group has done a few sessions it will realize for itself what kind of magic shift in emotions can take place.

Multiple-Role Playing: Multiple-role playing, mentioned earlier in this chapter as a means for quickly involving a large number of persons in a problem, also permits simultaneous examination of a problem by several subgroups. The preliminary steps are the same as in simple role-playing. Action in all of the subgroups begins at the same time and is cut at one time, usually on a predetermined time schedule. The experience can be analyzed by the group as a whole, or by individual subgroups and the results of the individual analyses reported to the entire group to compare and explore further.

When members are used to role-playing, each role-playing subgroup may, instead of reporting after analysis of the first scene, replay it or go on into a series of sequential scenes. Thus, when reports are made at the end of the replays or sequences, an extended variety of experience is available for study. However the advantages of multiple-role playing must be weighed against the loss of one of role-playing's major advantages—the obtaining of common experience by all members as a base for further analysis.

12. SALVAGING PROBLEM MEMBERS

In any normal situation few people can hold out for long against the wishes of the group. The feeling of separation becomes too strong. If they are ignored they feel as isolated, as set upon, as though they were actively opposed. They may fight for a while, but in the end they usually withdraw from the group or make peace on any terms which will let them save face.

Withdrawal may mean a serious loss to both the group and the person, and neither making peace nor compliance is enough. What everyone wants is to reduce the differences between the group and the resistant member so he will become a contributing one. This attitude obviously must be shared by all members if it is to succeed. In a member-centered group there is more than attitude to help them. Every stage of the process is geared to enhance the possibility of finding common ground. Every technique—even the evaluations at the end of the meetings—are so member-centered that most individual hurt is gone.

The contributions of all kinds of members are needed and it is important to weld them into a productive group before a divided pattern has become set. But it is also important to remember that the suggestions which follow are illustrative rather than comprehensive or infallible. From the psychological point of view, the apparent motives behind these, or indeed any, types of behavior may not be the real ones. Everyone has feelings and motives which he does his best to disguise. Particular behavior must be treated within the context of the particular situation and the individual

Absorb all kinds of members

involved. The following suggestions, however, when applicable, are constructive ways to show a member that the group needs his contributions and, to make them acceptable, wants to help change the behavior which is disturbing the other members.

Handling Nuisance Types

Just being part of a group that honestly wants to accomplish something and knows what that something is can be relied on to cope with most aspects of the nuisance type, for these flourish in the meetings classified previously as the Lambs-to-Slaughter. This is the group that doesn't fully know why it's coming together and is never given a chance to find out; in short, the group that has not bothered to make a problem census ahead of time or to agree on a mutual goal. The nuisance type of member, like the nuisance child, exists mainly in a situation where he hasn't enough to do. A job he's helped to plan makes sense to him and he soon ceases to be a nuisance.

But in the early meetings these nuisance types are almost bound to exist. The health of the group depends on letting them come out into the open rather than trying to suppress them.

The Pigeonholer and Hair-splitter

These types are enough the same to be lumped together. The Pigeonholer who wants to put things down in a notebook will get over that pretty rapidly. Faced with the blackboard and the fact that a copy of the recorder's notes will be sent him, he loses interest in his private notebook. But the one who wants definitions and who must ticket and package every bit of new knowledge before accepting it is a real nuisance, the more so in that he feels a great sense of superiority and virtue. "If it weren't for me . . ." he reasons.

This breed often turns up in a new group and requires considerable patience, understanding, and sometimes active support on the part of the other members. From the viewpoint of group health, this member needs to have his say, but not—unless an exact statement is necessary—his way. For the search for exact shades of meaning quickly becomes quibbling.

Why bother, then, to let him talk at any length? For this reason: most of us have to achieve some kind of prominence in a group. We have to feel important. The Hair-splitter operates the way he does because it was his way of getting attention in a *Robert's Rules* kind of session. So he should be allowed to talk and be important, even though it delays the group at the start. If he is thwarted, he will feel the group is against him. He will turn into a resistant member and be more than a mere nuisance. If he has his share of attention and respectful consideration early, he will then normally share the group decision, and as the group matures he will grow along with it.

The Eager Beaver and Explorer

These types, who grab at all new ideas, are apt to offer solutions whether they've given them any thought or not. But they don't have to have the patient consideration given to the Hair-splitter. They're usually good-humored and can be treated matter-of-factly. As the process of discussion forces them to back up their premature solutions, they learn to control themselves. Working with a group that is serious enough, they channel to productive ends that enthusiasm which made them such a nuisance at the beginning. They sincerely want the group to succeed and are the stuff from which fine working members are eventually made.

The Fence-sitter

With him it is important to know why he's sitting there. Either he has no confidence in himself and his own opinions, or he has a special reason for being sure he does not offend certain members of the group. He doesn't dare jump on one side or the other until he's sure of the verdict of those he considers key people. Even if all the members are new to him, he's likely to size them up quickly (as all of us do in a group), decide who's the dominant member, and wait for his cue from him.

There's little use in trying to get independent opinions from this member at the start, but the treatment that should produce them has to begin then. Obviously the permissive atmosphere has to come in here, the free, respectful attitude that should distinguish this kind of group. Try to get him to participate in the analysis phase of a problem—and let his opinions go. Other members can ask him if he has questions to raise or facts to offer in that analysis. If anything he says gets real consideration, he'll slowly gather courage and may begin to say what he thinks, not what he thinks he should think.

In office meetings of any kind, this member can become a useful contributor only if the boss makes it possible. In fact, any meeting that a superior in rank or status holds with his subordinates runs up against difficulties which only that superior can solve. The man who says no, and why, when he thinks no, is one of the most valuable workers any office or industry can have—if the superior in rank can take it. If he can't, he won't give more than lip service to group participation anyway. Even if he can take it and wants to, his actions have to prove again and again that he holds no resentment before any but the hardiest members will take him at his word.

The Wisecracker

He is the group clown, one of those who, whether they know it or not, are hunting importance, some means of making themselves stand out from the others. He has better hunting ground in a less serious group, in which the others are bored or aimless and welcome diversion. Should the group get absorbed in its work, the impatience with which the others view the wisecracking is enough to end it. The various methods we have described to help a group produce more will normally make him productive too.

The Superior Being

He is the not so common but very annoying member who looks down his nose at the whole business. Perhaps he didn't want to be part of the group in the first place ("I'm allergic to committees"), and agreed to join only because a friend persuaded him. He may represent his staff or feel it's his community duty. Whatever the case, he's apt to become the most resistant of all.

The group's best course is to find a problem, or an aspect of one, that interests and affects him. This may happen naturally; if it doesn't, specific effort should be made to slant the subject so that it catches his attention. He should be made to feel the group wants his opinions, regardless of how superior and indifferent he appears, and how irritating that appearance may be. The evaluation at the end may be used to arrest his interest, and also to give him notice that his indifference does slow things up. The observer can say,

"As you watched and listened today, X, I suspected that you had some ideas that would have helped us. For instance, on that point about . . ." Roused from the indifference he hoped he was getting away with, X probably comes through then, and later.

Silent Members

There are various types of silent members. The group's problem is to figure out the reason for that silence and act accordingly.

Some silent members are really constructive. They are:

1. The member who is not very vocal anyway and is in substantial agreement. He stays silent until some argument or proposed action upsets him and catapults him into the discussion. His silence does not need to disturb the group because it does not mean resistance or withholding.

2. The member who likes to listen to the argument and weigh all sides before he makes up his mind. There is a good possibility that he may bring forth a sudden and very workable solution to a problem.

Those who are destructive are:

1. The member who does not understand the problem or has not followed the action and hopes it will become clear if he just waits long enough. He doesn't like to confess his situation. If not cleared up, his misunderstanding may cause trouble later.

2. The member who is waiting for a moment to break in with a personal issue or some point which seemed good to him when it occurred. The discussion may long since have moved on but it is his idea. He liked it and he means to get it in. In the meantime he's lost the gist of discussion.

3. The normally vocal member who suddenly becomes silent. This is usually a form of resistance. He may not like the course the discussion is taking, or he may feel his contributions have not gotten the credit they should. He is the adult counterpart of the child who throws down his cards or ball or whatnot and stalks off, saying, "You're not being fair."

What's to be done about these silent ones? In the first place, it's well to recognize that contributions will always be uneven, varying with the intensity of interest, experience, and, of course, personality. But research has shown that everyone will be aggressive about something. In a continuing group it is worth while to find out what the something is to each of the members who are continually silent.

The next necessity is for the members to differentiate between the kinds who are sympathetic and interested and those who need help of one sort or another. Members generally are surprisingly quick at making this distinction, often as early as the second meeting. Those needing help require different kinds of treatment, depending on the reasons for their silence.

I want to be important too

The one who is silent because he is confused, and therefore embarrassed, finds the permissive atmosphere of this group his greatest support. The tone of respect given the opinions and contributions of all members creates in him a sense of freedom, not to mention courage. In the beginning the leader will probably have to set this tone, until the other members share the habit, with his techniques of throwing questions back to the group and interfering with the flow of discussion as little as possible.

The member who is silent because he's hugging his private idea to himself and waiting for an opportunity to unburden it is on vulnerable ground. The truth is he should not indulge himself. The blackboard and the other members' impatience at his coming in with a point long since canceled are usually enough to prevent repetition.

The member with a grievance should be given a chance to air it as soon as possible. If this should not occur, the evaluation at the end can be geared to letting him do so. Treat him with honest seriousness and the group will rewin a valuable member. This is also an occasion for role-playing (see Chapter 11) if the group can take the time.

Reporting on special assignments, being asked questions of fact about a matter known to be in the silent member's field, and role-playing are all techniques to help draw out the silent ones.

Direct questions are used only as a last resort, and then preferably by another member, not by the leader. Far better for a less reticent member to say, "I'm confused about . . . ," whether he is or not, if he guesses that to be the silent member's predicament. Throughout, it is every member's job, not just the leader's, to recognize such predicaments and act on them in a way that helps.

Destructive Members

Nuisance and silent types, given understanding and sensitive treatment, usually mature with the group process. They don't present a major problem.

But there are others, familiar to every meeting-goer, who can really destroy the essence of a group, for they destroy participation in the discussion. They pull in one direction—their own—and they try to pull others with them. They are usually articulate, potentially good members, and they must be coped with, or the group, as a group, is licked.

Someone has suggested that every member of a group should wear a large placard on his chest, stating, "I want to be important too." This is the key to handling the destructive members (indeed, all members). But no one can be important at the expense of the others, and the following types are. In general they don't realize what they are doing, so the thing here, once their need for importance has been partially gratified, is to make them aware.

The Dominator

He's dominated so long he simply can't stop and he's lost all realization of how he's affecting the other members. Most often he has a first-rate mind; he is quick and articulate. He sees the problem so rapidly that it's a bore for him to wait until the rest catch up. Once aware that he's preventing other contributions, he can be a top member. It takes some doing. Try the following:

1. Put the cards on the table at evaluation. This may have to be repeated several times, but that's okay. Your Dominator is fairly tough.
2. Role-play the situation (see Chapter 11).
3. Make him observer. (Remember our friend Joe Ellison, who talked for twenty straight minutes at the first meeting instead of starting a group evaluation. At the next meeting Joe's group put considerable emphasis on the way an observer should function. When Joe was made observer again he did the job well.)
4. Ignore his comments. As soon as he finishes, another member comes in with, "I was interested in what Hortense said a few minutes ago. . . ."

The Talker

He talks because he can't help it, a kind of neurotic situation. He, too, usually has no idea of how he's taking over the meeting. Apply the same treatment as for the Dominator.

The Blocker

Hear him out—maybe his plan is good; if it isn't, he must be given sufficient proof to get him to admit it. He wants attention; give it to him, and he should get over wanting it. If necessary, when he has stated his position, make him explain it. Then make him explain the explanation, and so on until his case is worn so thin that even he recognizes how the other members must feel about it. Then, having given him enough attention and rope to hang himself, ignore him and go on.

The Distractor

He breaks into the meeting because he either is really bored or has no interest in what the group is discussing. Or he isn't getting the prominence he wants and is taking revenge this way. Try to catch his interest in the problem, or make sure he helps choose the problem for the next meeting. Also, treat his arguments or point of view with more respect at later meetings. It takes two to make a distraction. If the group is serious, his efforts will die for lack of response.

Manipulator and Belittler

These both use the back door to get status and importance. Give them attention via the front door and they'll change as the group grows. If the Manipulator is seriously trying to use the group for his own ends, putting a spotlight on him and giving him attention is the group's best defense. Role-playing can help too.

The New Member

A new member may be the friendliest and most adaptable person in town but his newness makes him a problem per se: an unknown element which must be absorbed, a new force to be reckoned with. A brief introduction to the group is not enough. He automatically feels out of things, shy, and hesitant. (This will be his inner feeling whether he talks or is silent.) It is worth the group's while to take time out for explanations, almost to start again with him. He has to catch up on methods and techniques already familiar to the others. Role-playing may be a quick way to share his feeling. Above all, the members must realize that if they have been meeting for a time, no new member will easily be made a part of the whole. If they don't make him a part, he will keep the group from being as productive a unit as it should.

The Saboteur

The above types of members are problems but they believe in the group's goals and, in their own ways, contribute toward reaching them. The Saboteur is more sinister and, fortunately, rare. Also he is not salvageable. His purpose usually is to destroy the group or prevent its reaching its goals. He may use any type of nuisance or problem tactic and will probably vary them freely, in attempts to confuse or frustrate the other members. He may attempt to split the group by staging a whispering campaign or trying to develop a divisive clique. He may even try to capture the group and use it for his own ends. For this purpose he may try charm as a better weapon than domination.

The first difficulty with an example of this type is being sure that he is one. Is there solid evidence to distinguish him from a common manipulator or blocker? Or are members simply responding emotionally to his annoying tactics? Luckily, Justice Holmes has given us a simple divining rod: Is there a clear and present danger—to the group or its goals? If the determination is yes, the next question is: Will he be a greater menace inside the group or out? Through all this, the key to the group's defense, as most group members know but sometimes forget, is unity. If they work together closely, they can prevent the saboteur's making any headway, freeze him out indirectly or force him out directly, as they choose.

13. THE GROUP LEARNS TO PRODUCE

Just telling the members of a group that they should share the leader's responsibilities is about as productive as for parents to tell the adolescent members of a family to be more cooperative. It may be a relief to parents' feelings, but it won't get them anywhere. Before either group member or adolescent will respond, certain very human needs must be satisfied. Each has to know that his help is vital to the project. Most group members who have come along this far will take on a new kind of responsibility for the group's progress. How far "this far" is, from the point of view of those human needs, might be summed up as follows.

Their need: . . .	*Is satisfied by:*
to share the planning	problem census, defining goal, and choosing problems.
for respect and confidence	permissive atmosphere.
to feel their contributions count	attention and decision by agreement.
to be given actual responsibility for an impersonal measure of progress:	lack of domination, rotating leadership.
in discussion	blackboard and recorder.
in group performance	evaluation, post-meeting reaction sheets.

There is also another need: to recognize constructive patterns of behavior in a group, those which help to weld it into a working unit and to accomplish its purpose. These are specific functions that one or various members may perform in answer to the demands of the discussion. As they feel the situation calls for action, they come through with the kinds they believe appropriate. In the descriptive list which follows you may discern a resemblance to the less pleasant traits in group behavior already mentioned—and rightly, for even a constructive activity, if carried on too long or exclusively, can become a problem to the group.

The test is always provided by the situation itself. Every member should ask himself: What will this question do to the discussion? Will it bring out something important, or am I just talking to hear myself talk? Will putting in this remark really help anybody see the problem from a different angle? If I give up arguing over this minor point, will it help to reach a decision? Will this or that decision be satisfying enough so we will all do something about it, after the meeting?

Productive Group Activities

Some Activities Enrich and Organize Group Thinking

Initiating: suggesting new ideas, raising questions that push on the discussion. Group's best tool.

Clarifying: trying to make the meaning of various suggestions clear. It not only helps everyone but is the blackboard member's right-hand aid.

Elaborating: thinking of results and difficulties nobody else remembers (when not carried too far).

Integrating: summarizing and getting the group back on the point. Pulling related suggestions together. Often the key to a group solution or decision.

Some Activities Improve Analysis of Problems

Fact-seeking: asking questions (rather than making statements) which help bring out pertinent facts.

Analyzing: asking questions or making statements to bring out the fine points and the reasons behind the obstacles. Getting *below* the surface, in addition to Elaborating, which covers things *on* the surface.

Activating: thinking up situations or questions to bring out the knowledge of the other members. Behind-the-scenes activity. Boon to the silent member because it makes it seem urgent for him to contribute, too.

Some Activities Increase Group Solidarity and Progress

Encouraging: obviously an endearing trait in any member if he restricts it to honest encouragement.

Appreciating: keeping an open mind and modifying one's own viewpoints in the light of others which are better for the group.

Mediating: finding ways to reconcile clashing viewpoints.

Self-disciplining: suppressing the itch to lash out at other members. Keeping contributions on a reasoning basis. Pure gold.

Being group conscience: prodding the group to better or faster action. The quibbler's better nature.

To know, and recognize, these various activities actually helps members do a better job because people are quite willing to be constructive if they know how. For example, the discussion may be bogging down with the weight of facts and suggestions which really haven't anything to do with the problem. Somebody has to cut through the aimless talk and get it back on the subject, but the old hesitation at being the one to speak up, the old fear of sticking one's own neck out, holds everyone back.

To break in at such a moment used to be the chairman's function. Now it is also the members'. Recognizing which are the constructive, helpful activities, they are more willing to exercise them. The knowledge, in fact, has even shown the Explorer and the Eager Beaver profitable ways to use their energy and has given the Monopolizer pause. It prods the quiet members and strengthens those who lack confidence.

Have You Time for Analysis?

If the main job of the group is getting along well by now, it may not seem worth while to take time off for any kind of analysis. But even though the results are good, and are what the group was set up to achieve, results can always be improved. Participation can become still more effective.

The two following suggested methods for analyzing the group will not take much time from the subject matter. The first will not interfere at all with discussion; the second will only shorten it in part.

With the first method, the work on the problem continues as planned, but the observer limits his record for the evening to examples of both constructive and destructive types of member activity (with emphasis, needless to say, on the former). The group goes on with its work, forewarned of this special observation or not, as the leader likes. To make his job simpler the observer has a chart of these various activities on a good-sized sheet of paper, like the sample on page 87. He simply records each time (and with which type of activity) a member participates. Usually he can also manage to jot down on another piece of paper outstanding examples of constructive participation. At the end of the meeting, while the members are filling out their reaction sheets, he totals whatever participation record or records he has used and plans his comments on the highlights.

Then, keeping a weather eye out for emphasizing positive traits, he starts in: "I don't know whether you realize it or not, but the questions people ask in a group and the things they say can be classified. That's what I've been trying to do at this meeting. Of course, I've had to do it fast, and make a lot of arbitrary decisions. I've probably made a lot of mistakes too, but it will give you the idea."

If the observer can give each member blank copies of his chart at this point, they will be better able to follow his comments.

"The thing you'll find it hard to believe," the observer goes on, "is how many times* people actually do participate in a meeting. I couldn't believe it either, until I watched it happen. Of course, I can't begin to go into all of them, but I'll give you the high points. I'll start with you, Mr. Norcross [or "Ed," since the group is probably using first names by this stage in its meetings]. I thought you did a nice job on the whole, with—oh, well, maybe a couple of reservations. You initiated discussion three times. Remember how you came in there with that idea about . . . ? Then there were three times you integrated the discussion, pulled it together, and

---

* In a two-hour meeting the active members usually participate between thirty and forty times each.

SAMPLE OBSERVER'S SHEET

	Ed	Hortense	Joe	Andrew	Mrs. Buck	George	Virginia	Don	Roy	Total
Initiated	'''									
Clarified										
Elaborated	'''									
Integrated	'''									
Sought facts	''	''								
Analyzed		'								
Activated										
Encouraged	''	''								
Appreciated		'''								
Mediated	'									
Disciplined self	'									
Was group conscience										
Total										

Dominated	'''									
Manipulated										
Blocked										
Belittled										
Distracted		'''								
Split hairs										
Just talked										
Total										

twice you asked for facts. Five of your questions were analytical, like the time you asked why . . . ? Twice you encouraged other people to say what they had on their minds. Then there were three things I noticed you did just once. You mediated what might have turned into a time-wasting argument between Joe and Mrs. Buck. When people finished talking about . . . , no one seemed sure what to do next, and you activated the group by asking about. . . . The other time wasn't what you did, but what you didn't: from the way your face looked, you disciplined yourself. That was when . . .

This type of observation usually fascinates members

But about the middle of the meeting it got too much for you and you came in three times as a dominator. Remember? How did the rest of you feel about that?

"Hortense, the main thing I kept wondering about with you was whether you really cared very much about the problem. You did clarify once and elaborate once; and twice you checked facts and encouraged. But I also thought there were three times when you were a distractor. Am I right or wrong? Were you really interested?"

And so he goes through the list of members, winding up with, "Did I miss anything important?"

This type of observation usually fascinates members and gives them a completely new picture of how to do their share in helping a group get results. It's surprisingly simple to do, too, once the observer has learned the types of activity and knows how he has listed them on his sheet.

The other method requires no observer, is nowhere nearly so

revealing, and is admittedly less fun for the members. But it also works as a short cut to improved production. This divides the meeting into three parts. In the first, taking no more than ten or twelve minutes, the group lists the things that keep meetings from getting results or bore the members. In the second part of the session, they go on to the job of the evening, whatever it is. Then, in the third part, they take time to discuss the things they did themselves, that they'd all agreed people in meetings should *not* do.

Either of these ways helps the group to grow together and spurs it to better progress on subject matter. But perfection can't be expected, no matter how group-conscious the members feel. Meetings are bound to be uneven; a controversial problem will suddenly split the best group in half; a Dominator (or Blocker) may get excited and force his position on the others.

Yet by this time the group should have strength enough within itself to absorb such shocks and to reduce them almost to zero by evaluating each session. If it doesn't, the leader had better check on himself. Something of his original dominance as chairman (or just his natural dominance) may be hanging on. If the group isn't producing enough, or is not sharing the job, it may be because he is giving in to a lingering desire to be a boss.

14. DON'T BLAME THE EXPERT

The time is likely to come when even the most able and informed group needs outside help and decides to call in an expert.

Getting an expert is usually a matter of luck, one way or the other. He is asked (and often paid) to come and make a speech "on his subject." If he is entertaining the listeners are delighted—though some hours later they may realize that he didn't actually say anything that helped solve their problems. If he doesn't entertain, or his subject has nothing to do with their problem, they wait till he is well out of earshot and then say, "Well, that was a complete waste of time. We'll never do that again!"

Or there is that other situation, when the group goes to the expert.

In one instance ten couples, the parents of young children, began a study group with their county psychiatrist. A month later only four couples were going, and some of them were ready to drop out. Why? The parents not only organized the group in the beginning, but they picked the psychiatrist to run it. Their problems at home had not vanished, nor had their need for guidance. Nevertheless the attendance dwindled.

The fact was that they were getting no help. The psychiatrist was both expert and leader of the meeting. There was no doubt that he knew the subject; he was a reservoir of the kind of information they were after. But the members of the group were abashed, or silent, or just polite, as though they were making dinner conversation with a stranger. They waited for the expert to start the talk; they waited for him to guide them. He was a double authority, being both expert and leader, and they reacted as they used to in the classroom, facing a teacher. He, in turn, was clearly waiting for them to bring up their problems in a specific way so that he could give specific and appropriate answers. When they did not, he talked about experiences that might help them, or about points he thought important. It was a stalemate, but it was not the expert's fault.

Neither is it the fault of the expert when he comes to a group and makes a speech. The fault lies with the group. It is the job of the members, not the expert, to see that they get from him the information they need.

Before Meeting with an Expert

Calling in an expert is often a lazy way out of a predicament, in that it signifies the end of responsibility on the part of the members. But if this is not the case, an outside authority may lead them out of any number of problems.

Even so, it's better to start with the assumption that the group can find its own answers. Then, if that assumption proves false, the limits of what the members know will be unmistakable, and a more specific estimate of what it needs to learn will have been made.

The group should decide first just what kind of help it wants from an expert. The following may be suggestive:

1. Do you want facts that will take too long to find out or which you haven't the technical background to understand if you tried to look up the answers yourselves?

2. Do you want practical experience such as no one in the group has had?
3. Do you want help on your analysis of a problem?
4. Do you want answers on *how-to-do* something? Or do you want answers on *what-to-do?* Sometimes one expert can pro- how-to expert not an expert on the what. It's up to you to decide which, or you will expect a miracle instead of a human being.

If the group wants to make it easy for the expert, the basic questions should be in written form, not just in members' minds or in the mind of the one who is going to ask him to meet with the group. It will also help if he is told approximately how much the group already knows about the subject, and if each member has a copy of the set of questions to look at during the meeting.

Putting the requirements on paper will have another advantage. It will help the members decide just which of the experts they know (or have heard of) will best fill the need. Or if the right person has to be found by going through other people, written specifications will reduce the misunderstandings that almost always arise when a second person tries to explain a first person's meaning to a third.

All of this sounds and is harder than just inviting Jim Carson, for instance, the amusing person who immediately occurs to all of you, to make a speech. Even if the group finally decides that Jim Carson is the man, this preparatory work pays off. Since Jim will either be paid a whopping sum or be persuaded through the more ticklish route of social blackmail ("We can't pay you a thing, but we're all your friends," etc.), the group will want to get all it can. How does the group go about this?

Make the Expert One of the Group

Even when the leader has outlined the requirements for the expert, there is still the basic problem of how to handle him when he does come. He is an authority on his subject, and he will also be your guest. On both counts the group will be inclined to treat him with a polite but timid respect.

If he is put in the position of chairman as well, his dominance— and your timidity—will be reinforced. He may be an expert in his own field, but he's not necessarily an expert in drawing out a group.

The meeting is likely to wind up with the same stalemate that faced the child-study group.

To get around this unequal and wasteful situation, the first step amounts to "Stay as you are." Don't make the expert a chairman.* Don't try to make him a leader, in the terms we have been describing. Keep the leadership team as planned for the next meeting, and treat the expert as any new member meeting with your group would be treated. He's there, remember, to help with specific problems, to answer questions, not to make a speech; to facilitate group thinking, not to dominate it.

The temptation to enthrone the expert

The second step is to revise the group's attitude toward him so that although he has the respect any new member would be given it's not subservient or willing to accept everything he says as gospel. It may be gospel all right, but it may not be the group's gospel. He can only be as the members make him. Be sure that the group

* Twenty study groups in a county PTA had actually been written off as failures until they changed the setup and separated the functions of leader and expert.

is really getting what it thinks it is, without letting important angles of the problem go unexplored. Then and there, ask him questions which might give trouble later if they remain unanswered. Pin him down to the specific problem. Otherwise, someone later will come up with the valid argument that, "Well, what he said was all right for that situation, but ours is different."

Incidentally, the temptation to enthrone the expert and let him take over the meeting will be a strong one. After hours of struggling to find solutions to various problems, here is a man who sounds as though he knows the answers. It's a relief to relax and accept them. But if this is done the group is reduced from a creative, working unit to a submissive audience. You suppress your own valuable experience and accept without questioning. Next meeting, you will argue over what he said about this or that point, often wasting much time before you discover that what he said actually doesn't apply.

Set the Stage Ahead of Time

For the expert to assume the role of group member is a drastic change for him. He should have an explanation beforehand of what the change involves. Will he be willing to tackle the meeting on that basis? Will he mind cutting out his customary speech? Will he be content just to answer and ask questions?

If he's never heard of these group methods, the whole idea will probably interest him. If he has heard, he may be eager to see them in action. Even that skilled speaker Jim Carson will probably agree to take a shot at it. And there are others who know as much as, if not more than, Jim, who can be persuaded simply because they don't have to make a speech. Such a man, as well as any other potential expert, can be assured the group as a whole is responsible for helping him.

And responsible the group must be. Even though you've outlined what you want to know in the way of subject matter, it's only cricket for you to plan your own activity at the meeting so that it is easy for the outsider. He is not inclined to waste his time either, particularly if he is not being paid.

Since minutes of the last meeting and the usual formalities of *Robert's Rules of Order* have been discarded, the expert will at least not have to undergo that famous torture in which speakers have to sit through endless minutes, their eyes fixed in a glazed look of attention on the chairman who "makes a few announcements" and calls for reports of the subcommittees.

But he may have to undergo a subtler form of torture if the group does not make a special effort to stay on the subject, not just any subject but the particular one on which he can help. The blackboard member and the recorder can be primed for an extra awareness on this point, but the other members have to cooperate or it won't be enough. The leader can start the meeting by leading the expert directly into the problem: "Were any parts of our outline unclear? Are there some questions you'd like to ask us before we start the discussion?" Hit immediately at the things which necessitated his coming, and don't wander thereafter.

15. STIMULATING CHANGE

People who lead the kind of meetings this book discusses, and most of those who attend, often do so because they want to improve a situation. They may want better schools in their community, or better management in their organizations. Perhaps they want to persuade the city fathers to put street lights in their area. They may be working for a world government, or they may just want their committee to function more efficiently and produce better results.

Whatever the improvement, it has one thing in common with all the other desired improvements, no matter how big or how little they may be. If it is to be successful, it must change the thinking and habits of the people involved.

Stimulating that kind of change is one of the most difficult jobs yet discovered. Most people don't want to change. It is much easier for them to go along as they have been. Even if they think a change would be a good idea, their habits often won't let them accept it. It's almost as though they acted in accordance with that fundamental law of physics: a body at rest tends to remain at rest. Their own resistance to change is backed up by strong forces outside themselves, too. Changes usually upset community or organization tradi-

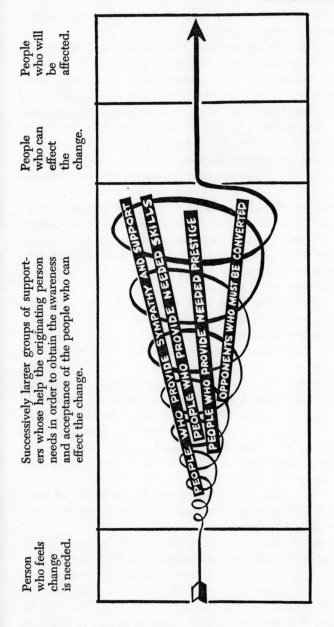

Person who feels change is needed.

Successively larger groups of supporters whose help the originating person needs in order to obtain the awareness and acceptance of the people who can effect the change.

People who can effect the change.

People who will be affected.

PEOPLE WHO PROVIDE SYMPATHY AND SUPPORT

PEOPLE WHO PROVIDE NEEDED SKILLS

PEOPLE WHO PROVIDE NEEDED PRESTIGE

OPPONENTS WHO MUST BE CONVERTED

tions or customs. They almost always conflict with some people's financial interests, power, or prestige.

Anyone who wants to accomplish changes in the face of such powerful forces must do a lot of thinking and planning. He probably needs help, sometimes a great deal of it. He and his helpers should know what resistance to expect and how to make people aware that changes are needed. Frequently they must be able, without losing sight of their main purpose, to modify their timing or some details of their goal so others will be able to accept them. When they have acquired a gun and ammunition they also have to know how to load, aim, and fire. And they need enough reserve ammunition to win the battle.

The process of creating change is a kind of spiral. It usually starts with one person who is able to help a few others understand, accept, and develop the needed ideas. Then that small group goes through the same process with a larger group, and so on until all those who need it are reached. Perhaps the design on page 95 will help show the nature of the process.

The spiral may have few loops in it, or many. A very simple example is in Chapter 6, where we discussed a leader who wants to help his group understand group development and use those principles in its own functioning. We suggested that he first discuss it with two or three of the group's influential members. That was the first loop of the spiral. The second and last was creating a leadership team. The team carried the change directly to the people who could effect it—in that simple case, the same persons who would be affected by it. At the other extreme are the men and women who are trying to change the world situation. Think how many thousands of loops their spiral must complete before it reaches the people who can put that change into effect!

All the way there must be an adjustment to the needs of those affected and a flexibility, a growth, that will absorb strength from the new people who join in support.

Here is a check list of questions intended to help hardy spirits examine their problems and plan their activities. It is divided roughly into four phases: appraising the situation; planning the change; putting the plan into action; cashing in—or checking out. The questions in italics are not general queries that summarize those that follow, but are questions that lead into a new phase or aspect of thinking.

CHECK LIST
FOR ANALYZING A SITUATION IN ORDER TO CHANGE IT

Appraising the Situation

Questions the Originator Should Answer

Exactly what do I want to accomplish?
For whose benefit do I want to accomplish it?
What are the advantages of that goal to me?
Any disadvantages?

How can I get all the facts about the situation?
How can I find causes, not stop at assumptions or rate things "good" or "bad"?
What forces favor the change? What forces oppose it?
What techniques of analysis can I use?
Do I need help from people who are specialists in using analysis techniques?

Who are the people to be affected by the changes I think are needed?
Are they aware of a need to make changes? To what extent?
Would they gain or lose anything from the changes? What?
What are the forces acting on them? Why do they behave as they do?
How will my goal and my attempts to reach it look to them?

Who are the people who can effect the changes?
What interests do they represent?
Are they aware of a need to make changes? To what extent?
Would they gain anything from the changes? What?
Would they lose anything from the changes? What?
What are the forces acting on them? Why do they behave as they do?
How will my goal and my attempts to reach it look to them?

Am I the logical person to carry the main burden?
In the early stages? In later stages?
Am I, or can I be, in an effective position?
Do I have, or can I get, the necessary knowledge and skill?

Who are the best people to give me the help I need?
What interests should be represented?
What special skills are needed? Which ones do I need at the beginning?
What support of position and prestige should I have?
To what extent are the people whose help I want interested in achieving this goal?
How would the change hurt or help each of them?
Can I count on them to help me develop a plan?

If not, how can I increase their interest and feeling of responsibility so they will want to help plan?

How can I help those who are resistant blow off steam if they need to?

Should I demonstrate the present situation to shock those who are apathetic?

Should I demonstrate the situation to be achieved, as an incentive to those who are passively interested?

How can I help each of my helpers answer for himself the first ten of these questions?

How can we as a group best answer the other questions I have answered?

Further Questions the Originating Group Should Answer

What kind of people are the individuals who can effect the changes needed?

What are their prejudices and traditions? Their interests? Their habits and values?

What effects will pressure for the change probably have on their beliefs and behavior?

How can we cope with their reactions in ways which will reduce their resistance?

How can we make them aware of the need for changes?

How can we help them understand how the changes will benefit them?

How can we introduce the new ideas so they will want to try them?

Are some of them favorably enough disposed to help do the planning?

How can we encourage and support them as they try the change?

Planning the Change

What plan of action can we use that will contribute to our goal by its nature as well as by what it can accomplish?

What are the steps we must go through?

What is a realistic time schedule?

What are the details of the first step?

How, when, and where do we start?

How do we organize to carry out the plan successfully?

Do we need a staff and facilities?

How can we provide them?

Have we provided for good communication among ourselves?

At what points should we appraise our progress and, if necessary, revise our plans?

How do we go about making appraisals of progress?

Are there any key actions that will indicate success or failure?

To what extent will they give us adequate information?

What else do we need to cover?

What techniques can we use?

Can we determine them ourselves or do we need a specialist to help us?

To what extent may it be helpful and feasible to include in this activity people who can effect the changes needed?

How can the group explore the probable consequences of its key decisions and planned actions?

Do we need practice in carrying out any parts of the plan?

What do we need to know about the way groups function?

About helping groups function most effectively?

Do we need to know how groups reach decisions?

Putting the Plan into Action

Once we have started on our plan, are we keeping on our course, not going down some byway or concentrating on some minor aspect?

Are we taking advantage of the knowledge our analyses gave us?

Are we keeping our communication good?

Are we pushing our activity at the right speed? Do we know when to initiate the big push? Are we ready to supervise it properly?

Do we know when and how to conclude it successfully?

How can we diagnose causes if our group action becomes inefficient?

Is the goal we determined still what we want to achieve?

Did we have all the facts? Were they correct? Did we accept as facts assumptions which were incorrect?

Was our estimate of the situation correct?

Were there weak spots in our plan? What were they?

Did we fall down in our execution of the plan? When? How? Why?

Did we fail in meeting unexpected situations? When? How? Why?

Can we answer these questions ourselves or do we need help from others? What others? People affected by our plan? Technical experts?

How can we determine, and take, effective action to correct weaknesses in our performance and improve our progress?

Are there some aspects of our goal we must modify or sacrifice in order to achieve the rest?

What effects do additional or better understood facts have on our plans?

What is our present estimate of the situation?

What can we do to prevent recurrence of our errors in carrying out the plans?

How can we improve our ability to meet unexpected situations?

What lessons have we learned which will assure us that our evaluations are complete and sound?

Cashing In—or Checking Out

When we have completed our plan, have we accomplished our goal?

Were we wrong in believing we could reach our goal? Why?

Have changes in the situation made it too difficult for us to reach? Why?

What forces are now for us? Against us? What can we salvage? Can we still achieve part of the goal?

Should we wait for a better time? When is it likely to be? What should we do in the interval to strengthen ourselves?

Do we want to maintain our gains or spread them? To what extent? In either case, who are the people we still need to convince?

What are their reactions to what we have accomplished?

How can we make them aware of the need and develop their acceptance of our accomplishments so far?

How can we get their interest and participation?

Who are the people outside our immediate area of interest who are affected by our activities?

How can we learn their reaction to our accomplishments?

What effect are they likely to have on our activities?

Are there people or organizations who are a threat to our accomplishments?

What do we need to do about them?

How shall we select future or supplementary leaders?

What qualifications should people have to be capable of replacing us as leaders or augmenting us? What available people have them?

What do we need to do to stimulate their interest so they will be willing to assume responsibility?

What other people are willing to become leaders? Which of them can be given sufficient capability by training and further experience?

What do we need to do to make them qualified?

How do we know when to stop, merge, or delegate?

Do we have any reason to continue to exist as a group?

Is our goal secure enough so there is need only to protect it from, or adjust it to, newly arising forces?

Can some other group do that as well as we?

Is there any other reason to affiliate with another group?

Do we want to retain any nucleus or records?

16. LEADING A ONE-MEETING GROUP

If a group is called together for one meeting only, how much use can it make of these methods? How far can the leader go in helping it to have discussion on a free basis?

Perhaps a difficulty has suddenly arisen in an office and Mr. Jones gets a telephone call from his superior, asking him to call various people together to decide what to do about it. Or a problem has come up in the Community Chest office which requires an immediate decision from certain key figures in the community. One meeting will suffice in either case. Can these new methods help at that meeting?

The answer depends somewhat on the experience of the members, but far more on the conviction and skill of Mr. Jones. Let us assume this kind of meeting is new to the members but that the leader has been working regularly with a small group that has been using these techniques. He knows the change in participation and the results that can follow when the members feel free to contribute and reach a solution through agreement rather than by voting. He knows what can be done by way of really shared production—if there is a series of meetings.

But he does not have several meetings. He has only one, made up of members who are used to a traditional, chairman-controlled session. What does he do?

He makes a choice, of course, and in making it he may find the chart on page 103 useful. On it he sees (to bolster his own experience and conviction) that group production increases as the leader lessens his control. He would like to function as a stimulator, to permit production to reach the highest point, but in one meeting that is out of the question. He has to be content with the middle course, in which production will rise from mere support of his opinions to some real participation—if he is capable of helping it do so.

Proceeding on that halfway basis, he has the meeting room set up in the same way that it would be for any free-discussion, small group meeting: chairs arranged in a U, closed by a blackboard or an easel. He will serve as his own blackboard member, and though he needs to ask someone to record the gist of the meeting, he has no observer.

The group participates, but he controls. A meeting of this type may have a detailed agenda which provides automatic time limits. If it does not, he may want to set time limits on the various phases of discussion as both a control and a prodding device.

The opening of the meeting finds him, perforce, in control of the group and of the situation. After the round of introductions (if necessary), he explains that he is going to try to conduct this meeting differently from those the members are used to attending. Since they are there to pool their knowledge and ideas about the problem, he feels they can reach better solutions by working together than by waiting for his lead. To the best of his ability, he is going to try to turn questions back to them so they can come up with the answers.

The group's goal has been handed them; so, too, has the problem for which they are to find a solution. At this point, then, the leader puts the problem on the board (or easel paper), pauses to make sure all the members have the same understanding of it, and then puts the heading "Related Facts" at one side, and "Obstacles" at the other. Then he starts his first questions to help the group bring out what needs to go under each of these headings.

Here, in spite of his opening remarks, the members will try to make him chairman, since that is the situation they are used to, by getting him to answer questions. If he knows the subject and has definite opinions about it, he may have difficulty in resisting the temptation to answer. His solution is to keep that impulse under control and toss the question back to the group for clarification, "So I can get it on the board." If he persists and keeps reminding the members that the suggestions he presents are simply to give them focal points for discussion, they will eventually realize that he means what he has said and begin seeking their own answers.

But don't expect that happy cooperation to last. One member or another gets carried away with his own angle on the problem and wants to monopolize the discussion. Another wanders off the subject,

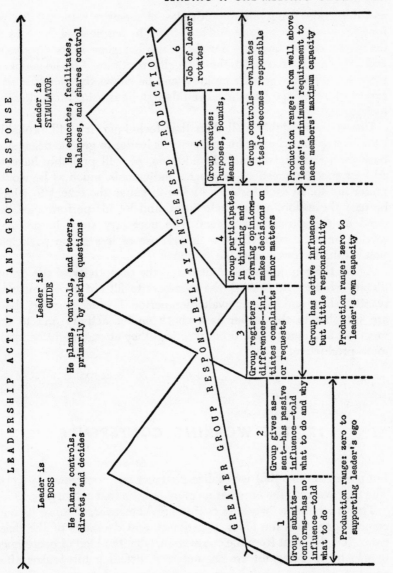

LEADERSHIP ACTIVITY AND GROUP RESPONSE

Leader is
BOSS

He plans, controls,
directs, and decides

Leader is
GUIDE

He plans, controls, and steers,
primarily by asking questions

Leader is
STIMULATOR

He educates, facilitates,
balances, and shares control

GREATER GROUP RESPONSIBILITY—INCREASED PRODUCTION

1

Group submits—
conforms—has no
influence—told
what to do

Production range: zero to
supporting leader's ego

2

Group gives as-
sent—has passive
influence—told
what to do and why

Production range: zero to
leader's own capacity

3

Group registers
differences—ini-
tiates complaints
or requests

Group has active influence
but little responsibility

4

Group participates
in thinking and
forming opinions—
makes decisions on
minor matters

5

Group creates:
Purposes, Bounds,
Means

Group controls—evaluates
itself—becomes responsible

6

Job of leader
rotates

Production range: from well above
leader's minimum requirement to
near members' maximum capacity

and the leader longs for some display of member responsibility or for a leadership team to rescue him. Since he has neither, he looks at his watch, determines how far the group has gone in its discussion and whether he dares let the difficulty continue. For he alone is responsible for the group's progress and he knows the members will expect him to shape its course even though he is using a questioning technique.

Unless he is highly skilled in that technique, he will probably have to step in and exert his authority as leader to get the discussion back on a productive track. In addition, he will probably have to address specific questions to specific individuals, much as he would prefer not to. In each instance he has to gauge the extent to which he uses these dominating techniques, and let his performance depend on the situation he faces. The necessary steps in problem solving must be covered even though use of less group participation results in fewer valuable solutions.

Again, the requirements of time and the receptivity of the group dictate whether he can ask the members to fill out a post-meeting reaction sheet and have an evaluation period. If at all possible, these are valuable to the leader as a check on his activity and to the members as a clue to how other meetings they attend might be made more productive.

17. THE WORKING CONFERENCE

Let us say at once that we realize planning any conference is work. The type we describe here has no monopoly on that activity.

This is labeled a "working conference," however, because its outcome depends on the ideas, experience, and decisions of the delegates. It is different from the convention, from the kind of conference in which the delegates are an audience, listening to speaker after speaker. If the delegates run into the thousands, certain of these techniques can be adapted, but any detailed suggestions for handling that large a conference lies outside the scope of this book.

If the object in holding a conference is to pool information and thinking to the end of delegate-made decisions, then the working conference should come closest to answering those needs. It is based on this general pattern:

1. Delegates select the problems.
2. Decisions are made by delegates in small face-to-face groups through free discussion.
3. Delegates meet periodically in general sessions to report decisions of small groups, make over-all decisions, and keep in touch with the work of all groups.
4. Experts (from within and without body of delegates) work right with groups and are available for panel discussions if necessary.

It would not be possible in one chapter to give more than a skeleton planning program. Not even a book could anticipate all the details, the hazards, the surprises, the irritations, the last-minute crises, the complaints—and the satisfactions—ahead. All we hope is to give you, the steering committee, as workable a guide as possible for planning a working conference.

Preliminary Activity

Delegates will be coming from ten, fifty, or a hundred groups located throughout a county, state, or the nation. They may be representing small business at a trade association meeting, or chapters of a professional society. Perhaps they come from branch offices of a large corporation or from the locals of a trade union. They may be volunteer workers, or paid workers in a volunteer agency. Or they may represent only themselves—individual scientists or educators. Whatever the group, its members will probably be so widely dispersed that the steering committee can only find out what they want to discuss by mail.

After the first "feeler letter" to determine interest in a conference, another letter should go out, the returns from which will provide the cornerstone for building the whole conference. Since it belongs to the delegates, not to the planners, what do the delegates want to get from it? What are the problems they want to work on?

This basic letter must serve two purposes, plus a possible third:

1. To get a yes or no answer on probable attendance.
2. To provide a problem census on the basis of which the discussion groups will be formed.

3. (Possible) To get the names of the in-the-field delegates who, because they have had success in working out a particular problem, can be recruited to serve as experts.

The letter needs to emphasize the importance to those who are planning this conference of knowing which problems the delegates wish to discuss. Also, make it clear that all the mechanics of the conference depend on their stating their preference as quickly as possible. It will probably help the delegates if they are given some possible problem areas (keeping them general rather than specific). Set up the letter so that they can check their preferences and urge them to write in any others they wish which are not listed.

If it seems advisable, ask each whether he has found a satisfactory way to solve a problem which he thinks others may find helpful (those potential experts). And last, this basic letter had probably better carry an explanation of what kind of conference this is going to be. It will not be the last time an explanation is necessary, but it should be the first.

No matter how carefully the letter is worded, the returns may be small and slow coming in. Even so, base the preliminary conference plans on whatever returns do come. They won't constitute a scientific sample but they will show the thinking of people interested enough to reply. List discussion groups for each problem in which the delegates show significant interest—particularly for each batch of written-in problems which are closely related. If few of the returns show concern about problems which you, the steering committee or the high command, thought paramount, skip yours, not the delegates'. This is, remember, their conference.

At first glance it may seem impossible to set up enough groups, or delegates within each group, for each problem. But a second glance usually shows that several seemingly different definitions of a problem are, in essence, enough the same to justify putting them into one group. No two people see a problem from quite the same angle, as we have mentioned before, but the angles can be made to fit together well enough to make a whole.

Check the possible list of groups with the possible number of delegates. For the best discussion, a group should not include more than twelve or thirteen discussants, or fewer than five or six. With an observer and recorder, the range would be from seven or eight to fourteen or fifteeen. Dividing the expected number of delegates by ten will give a rough index of the number of groups for which to provide time, meeting places, and leadership teams.

If the number of desired subjects varies considerably from the number of expected groups at this point, don't worry about it. Think in terms of the maximum number of groups, and remember that when the conference starts, flexibility will be a cardinal virtue. At the last minute some groups that are too small will have to be combined with others or dissolved so their members can discuss more urgent problems elsewhere. Some groups that are too large may have to be split. Just provide enough facilities and team members, and plan to take a sleeping pill the night before registration.

D-Day Minus 90

It is now none too soon for the steering committee to split up into three subcommittees, since there is too much work ahead for one commitee to cope with it all. Other subcommittees may also be important for you, but these three—to provide physical facilities, to provide experts, to provide and train leadership teams for the discussion groups—must function ahead of time to make this conference a success. These three subcommittees must work simultaneously.

Each subcommittee obviously has to start by answering certain basic questions:

1. What are our requirements?
2. How much can we spend?
3. What people (or facilities) are available within our limits of budget and requirements?
4. How do we go about getting the data we need on people? On places?

Providing Physical Facilities

Since poor physical facilities and arrangements can ruin the most promising conference, here is a check list of the key items.

Small-group meeting rooms:

    Well lighted and ventilated, free of outside noises.

    Tables to provide U-shaped grouping with width no less than two-thirds of length.

    Blackboard, four feet by eight feet, or larger, and easily reversible (or equivalent space provided by easels), placed so members' attention is away from source of outside light.

Poor physical facilities can ruin the best conference

Comfortable chairs.

Ash trays.

Preparatory arrangements:

Identification cards if members do not know each other (or experts do not know them).

Arrangements at registration desk for registering members by discussion groups.

Handouts giving members all information they need about conference arrangements, physical facilities, recreational facilities (if pertinent), and calendar of events.

Mimeographing materials, arrangements for getting reports to delegates quickly, and, if necessary, a loud-speaker.

Post-meeting reaction sheets.

Large meeting room:

Size adequate for expected group, but not over-large.

Good visibility and acoustics.

As little separation as feasible between platform and members, but an adequate area visible to all for role-playing demonstration if one is to be used.

Maximum possible amount of blackboard space, distributed about the room so all members can read what is written.

Providing Experts

At the usual conference, the speakers are almost the first and main consideration. Success or failure often depends on their drawing power.

At a working conference, what experts are there join the delegates in their discussions to supply special information when it is needed. They should also be available to take part in panel discussions, should these prove desirable.

This difference in function makes a difference in the steps taken by the committee to secure experts. Its job is not to find speakers, but to find people with appropriate information; if necessary, one for each group. The planners have to be guided not only by limitations of money, but by those set up by the pattern of this conference.

Big-name speakers (a tempting and automatic source of publicity) are not ruled out as experts—if you can afford them. But they may rule themselves out when they understand that they will not hold the platform, klieg-light position. Or they may be captivated and more than ordinarily interested by this approach, yet be unable to devote the time required to stay with a group throughout the conference. (In that case, take them for at least some of the small group discussions—not at the beginning, when the group is trying to get at the core of the problem, but in later small meetings.) If the conference is a one-day affair, such experts are more likely to be able to meet with the groups, and the job of finding them is simplified.

On the other hand, if big names don't mean much for your purposes, why not canvass the lists of delegates first? Check with the problem-census returns and consider the occasional person who may have found a working solution to some of the problems (see problem census, page 35. Consider those the steering committee members know or know about.

The general field of the conference will necessarily determine the background the experts must have. Is it education? Religion? Community work? A specific science or industry? Labor relations? Union activity? Business management or governmental administration? Law? A charity? Politics? Or is it a field which from time to time reaches out into another field? In case the delegates cannot supply the information, what people in outside fields have the really constructive ideas your organization wants? Which are within reach, geographically and financially? Of those, which ones will be willing to work on a shoulder-to-shoulder basis with the group? Which would be willing to be on call, in case a sudden need arises?

Whatever the choices, make sure that you help those experts by explaining ahead of time your needs (see Chapter 14) and the—to them—unusual requirements of this conference. Then have a brief preconference session with the experts, perhaps during registration or lunch the first day, to talk over together the roles they will play.

Providing Leadership Teams

Unlike the experts, the members of the leadership teams—leader, observer, recorder, and blackboard member—will not be determined by the nature of the discussion problems. Pick them from the members in sufficient number to equal the expected number of groups. Better still, more than equal. Provide extra members for the preconference training session, and a recorder for the large general meetings. Then, when the inevitable occurs and some have to drop out at the last minute, the substitutes have been trained and can step in.

Obviously those serving the groups in this leadership capacity should be intelligent, conscientious, and adaptable. They should also have enough self-confidence to be willing to tackle a new job. But any organization is full of people who feel they meet these qualifications—or of loyal followers who will claim they do. How can the planners, at a distance, select the best?

The answer, of course, is that they cannot. They have to go by the best advice they can get and count on the preconference training session to do the rest. Certain general qualifications may help:

Choosing leaders:

Try to avoid those who like to dominate, be in the limelight, or who are in a position of power. It is difficult for any of these types to submerge their own personalities and they will probably wreck any hope of free discussion. Like the boss at staff meetings, they can't help but be treated with too much deference. If, for the sake of future peace and cooperation within the organization, these powerful members must be accepted in some position of importance, don't make them leaders. Give them conference jobs outside the discussion groups, or, if they must have positions within the group, make them experts. Thus they will be able to share their experience without seeming to direct the outcome of the group thinking. In any case, try to scatter the important delegates throughout the groups.

Choosing observers:

The best observers are delegates who are enough interested in methods of group development so they do not too much mind staying out of the problem discussion. They also should be broad-gauged people who can steer clear of details and personalities.

Choosing recorders:

This is a less rewarding job in itself than any of the others on the leadership team, since it usually keeps the member completely out of both discussion and evaluation. If any funds can be devoted to these activities, it's a good idea to pay stenographers or stenotypists so that delegates will not have to perform that chore.

On the other hand, to take stenographic notes of the first stages in a discussion group might be sheer waste of money. It takes time for a group to get into the swing of discussion and to get "on the beam." It might be good practice (and more economical) to let a member take these notes for the first session of the small group and have a stenographer report after the first break.

Choosing Blackboard Members:

The discussion will benefit, of course, if this member is someone who can separate the significant points from the minor ones in a discussion. Long-distance guessing on this is hopeless. As with the other team members, you have to base your choice on what you can pick up from local sources—and pin your hopes on the preconference training sessions for the leadership teams.

In general, if there are delegates who have already served successfully as leadership team members, should they be used? Probably not, if there are enough likely new candidates. There are several reasons for this. The more members who get a little training and experience in these jobs, the better. Experienced people will be especially valuable as regular group members and a superb reserve for leadership teams in emergencies. Keep them in reserve, but be sure to tell them why they have not been picked and ask them to be ready to step in as replacements.

When you have picked the members you would like to have on your leadership teams, send each a letter. Explain the functions of the team and its members. Ask each to serve in a specific capacity. Tell them also that the job will require their coming a day ahead of the conference for a training session. You cannot emphasize too much the importance of their being at that session.

The chance of discussion groups being wrecked by untrained leadership teams is very high. If some do not turn up for the training session, use your reserve line-up of members with experience, rather than take the chance of wrecking your conference. The most serious chance of failure in this type of conference comes from skimping on the training of leadership teams. The steering committee should not be afraid to take the time to train team members.

D-Day Minus 30

Send out any source material you wish delegates to have as background for discussion, and make your plans for training leadership teams.

Training Leadership Teams

Teams for a large conference have been trained in one evening, but the team members are usually the first to realize that they should have had more time. Once the conference starts, the weakness becomes apparent even to the delegates.

It takes many regular meetings for a small group to grow together and work productively. Obviously the small groups which function in a conference cannot reach that stage in one, two, or even three days. But they can accomplish minor miracles if those in the key positions in each group—the leader, observer, blackboard member, and recorder—have had a day of intensive training before they meet with the group. The main requirement for leadership team members (after learning what their functions are) is practice, and a lot of it. Without it, they give the groups they lead only a fraction of the help they might.

In Appendix II we suggest a training plan which consists of a series of very short meetings held in one large room and several small ones. Some of these are practice sessions in which three leadership teams comprise a working unit. Each team in turn leads a brief meeting, with the other teams serving as the remaining members of the group. This gives all the teams trial runs and a chance to profit by watching other team members doing the same thing. Then together they all evaluate what they have done. With this experience behind them, the teams have a real feeling of security in the conference proper and can help their groups produce valuable results.

Recruiting a Training Staff

Like any other training session, this one requires a staff and someone in charge, a leader who knows these methods of group development and has had experience with them.

The leader, in turn, needs experienced people to help him with the separate teams, so that as the groups go off to separate rooms each has a trained person who can help, suggest, criticize, and answer all the questions bound to come up. These trainers need not have had experience in training for a conference, but they should have served sufficiently on the leadership teams of small groups to know both the techniques and the attitude necessary.

Where are you going to get these people to do the training?

Of course the preferred source is within your own organization —and it is a very likely source. The methods we have been describing in this book may be new to you; hence you may not realize how widely they are being used or how unnew they may be to your delegates. So check throughout your own organization first.

Then inquire outside your organization. The leader and his staff of trainers do not need to know about the problems of your organization for this purpose; what they need to know is how leadership teams function. If, on inquiry, you fail to turn up people with this experience—and the skill of translating this experience to others— write to the National Education Association, Washington, D. C.

D-Day

The time at this kind of work conference needs to be divided between general sessions and small face-to-face working discussion groups. Lunch and/or dinner can be used to give interim reporting or to highlight important points. The final session needs to be reserved for summarizing and general evaluation.

A Sample Timetable

As an example of what can be done in even part of a day, here is the over-all plan used by a county-wide PTA for a conference of the officers and committee chairmen of the local PTAs. This timetable can easily be used as is, or adjusted to special needs of a longer conference.

1:30 to	2:00	Registration.
2:00 to	3:00	Opening general assembly: greetings by the president; demonstration of group discussion; explantion of new method; role-playing a bad and a good meeting.
3:00 to	6:00	Small group meetings on problems selected by participants, with each group evaluating its own group process.
6:00 to	6:30	Recess.
6:30 to	7:30	Dinner.
7:30 to	8:00	Report on highlights of afternoon meetings.
8:00 to	9:30	Continuation of same discussion groups, but with emphasis in each group on what the group is to do about carrying out the decisions made during the afternoon.
9:30 to	10:30	Closing general assembly: final reports from the discussion groups; general evaluation of the conference; conclusions.

Registration

This migraine-headache chore we mention not because the social scientists have discovered any way to simplify it, but because it is an occasion which can be used for other purposes as well.

For example, here is the way it was used by the county-wide PTA Institute to which we have just referred and will refer frequently. In the first place, as the delegates walked up the broad steps of the entrance hall, they were met by an enormous poster which listed the problems to be discussed. Each problem, worded as a question, had a number before it, and each of the hundred and thirty-five delegates either confirmed his previous choice of problem, by number, or chose one. This was necessary because, though letters had been previously sent out as a problem census, this was not a closed conference. People came who had not registered ahead of time. They, too, needed to choose which problem they wanted most to discuss. Another chart listed the room number for each discussion group.

Second, the delegates were given a calendar of the day's events. This was in no sense the usual agenda. It was rather a combination of schedule and program and included reference material (names, a map of the county, etc.) which they might find useful.

Last, this registration corridor provided the most eye-catching time and place to exhibit material which even at a working conference may be important for the delegates to have.

The Kickoff Session

This conference started, as any presumably must, with a speech of welcome by the president. However, he kept it short, and kept equally short his explanation of how the sessions would proceed: with work and real participation by all members. He ended with the fact that a short skit would follow to illustrate his words, then left the front of the room. Eight members of the planning committee brought their chairs to the front, arranged them in rows, and played a typical committee meeting. At their head was the chairman, familiar to all of us, full of little jokes at the start and a dictator thereafter—the kind who can spot a maverick and rule him out of order almost before he gets to his feet.

There was the timid member, too frightened to speak, and the less timid who began but was promptly outvoiced by another, who kept coming in at intervals, like a Greek chorus, insisting on his point ("Everything depends on better equipment in the cafeteria!"). And the conscientious objector, and the one who whispers her ideas behind her hand to her nearest neighbor but wouldn't think of saying them aloud.

A commentator stood at one side, explaining the bad points—quite unnecessary, as it happened, and hardly to be heard over the laughter. Then the chairs were rearranged and the same subject was handled with all members participating, a decision reached, and the techniques of the leadership team played out for all the delegates to see and understand.

The first skit took ten minutes, the second fifteen. The planning committee had roughed out these skits in one session, literally feeling their way and acting as the general situation indicated. With no more preparation than that, they gave the whole conference not only fun but a startling vitality and eagerness, which, we feel, could not have been duplicated in any other way. Though this was not a large conference, this type of springboard can be used for any size group—with microphones if the room is very large.

At a different conference, one of about forty-five people, the members of the three leadership teams started a "good" demonstration discussion of one of the meeting's important problems. Very soon the audience began to participate to an extent that allowed the leader to say, "There are some people near me who say this group is too big. Shall we break it up now into smaller groups?" This they did, and went on from there.

Buzz sessions (see Chapters 9 and 10) can also be used to start discussion and thinking. They may or may not be combined with panel discussion or a single speaker, as the case requires.

The opening session is the time to make clear, once again, what this type of conference is to be like, and to inject into it some part of the dynamic spirit which, it is hoped, will carry through into the small groups. (It is not the time for reports and business, consideration of bylaws, etc. Granted that these are an evil not to be avoided at every conference, set up a separate session for them. Do not bog down the conference at the start or the final general session which needs to pool decisions and evaluate the past performance.)

Small Group Meetings

We assume that these will make up the working part of the conference and will follow the general pattern outlined earlier in this book. If the groups are to meet only once or twice, one variation would be useful: have the observer make a brief evaluation as early in the first meeting of each group as poor member (or leader) behavior warrants. This is a quick way to salvage time which might otherwise be wasted by the members in their attempt to come to grips with the problem and the method of discussion.

Use One Meal

Even the most zealous conferees need to relax after the small group sessions. But a report of what is going on at the various groups can be given at one meal a day—if it is done well and lasts not more than fifteen or twenty minutes. Often enough, delegates have difficulty making a choice of discussion group; at least one other seems to be almost as appealing, and since they can be in only one group at a time, they are curious about what is going on elsewhere. The fifteen-minute report is a quick technique for satisfying that curiosity.

In the interval between the small group sessions and the meal, leave time enough for the leadership teams to pick out the highlights of that session and turn them over to someone who can digest them enough to make a report. The report can be followed by buzz sessions, if the delegates wish.

At the PTA Institute, this report was made with astonishing success. As the delegates ate, they were suddenly interrupted by what seemed to be, for all purposes, a radio announcer: "This is Station WPTA, your wandering reporter," and so on.

Final get-together

Final Get-Together

Whether this takes place at the end of a one-day conference, or at the end of a longer one, considerable time must be allowed for the last general session. It must also move with the greatest possible speed, for the delegates are tired. It must include the final pooling of reports, any joint decisions needing to be made, filling out the post-conference report sheets (similar to PMRs), any plans for future meetings and plans for getting recommendations put into action, etc. Try not to schedule small group sessions the same evening, if they can be avoided.

Buzz sessions may be necessary if there is disagreement on decisions reached in separate groups. And if no agreement can be reached in the time at hand, disagreements must be included as statements of minority opinion in the final post-conference report. Whether the conferees want a copy of the report must also be decided.

In any case, careful planning must be done ahead of time for this final session so that not too much ground has to be covered by delegates who have part of their minds on catching planes or trains and have already, it is hoped, worked to capacity.

18. MISAPPLICATIONS AND MISCONCEPTIONS

Misapplications

Although member-centered meetings can serve productively in many situations they must be used within their limitations. At one extreme, for example, may be a group whose constitution requires certain formal rules of procedure. In that case no alternative exists to suspending those rules during discussion, reaching decisions in a problem-solving way, and then ratifying those decisions with a traditional vote. At the other extreme are situations in which people may try to use member-centered meetings as therapy groups. The meetings we discuss in this book can help solve group problems, not individual ones. They can only be valuable to a person needing psychological aid if his participation in the group activity helps him modify some overt evidences of his trouble or stirs him to seek professional help.

Between these two extremes are circumstances in which member-centered meetings are good for some purposes but not for others. For example, an executive can find excellent uses for them within his organization, as discussed in Part V, and he may be responsible to a board of directors which itself uses member-centered meetings in making policy. But the hour-to-hour problems which arise in carrying out a program or conducting everyday business require individuals with authority to make prompt decisions.

Leadership

Researchers have found very few personal qualities that are universally essential for leadership. They have concluded that a group free to pick its own leader chooses the member it believes best suited to carry the responsibilities then most important to help it reach its goals. Hence, new leaders arise to meet new situations, or informal ones appear when a formal head does not represent the members but they cannot remove him.

When, as another example, buzz groups are set up, they are without leaders, but leadership develops in them almost immediately. An excellent device for demonstrating the variety in this process is to have the members analyze the growth of leadership in their own buzz group, then compare their experience with those of their cohorts in the other groups.

Acts of leadership continue to be just as essential as they always have been. Without them few groups accomplish much or even go on existing. Whether the leader performs all of these acts himself or shares some with the members depends on the group's purpose and operating methods, as the chart "Leadership Activity and Group Response" on page 103 highlights.

Continuity of leadership is also as necessary as ever. Whether the group shares the function as in a member-centered meeting, or has *a* leader, as in most hierarchical situations, effectiveness declines quickly if there is a hiatus in leadership acts. Changing of leadership is apt to have a similar effect, particularly when a leader is replaced, unless the new head demonstrates capability promptly.

The No-Method Fallacy

The lack of accomplishment of groups which succumb to the no-leadership fallacy is matched by that of others that discard the agenda of a traditional meeting but don't replace it with a flexible problem-solving method of their own. Getting people together with great good will but no concept of where they want to go or how, leads nowhere more often than flattery is supposed to.

The Conformity Problem

In recent years considerable attention has been focused on the tendency of many people to yield to community and organizational pressures which turn them into conforming robots, reluctant to exercise initiative or develop their individual ideas.

Member-centered meetings are invaluable forums for resisting these pressures. A group that respectfully examines all viewpoints gives each member a favorable chance to bring others to his thinking, whether it is conformist or not. To seek an integrated solution, in which all members take into account the other members' basic needs, is the antithesis of conformist pressure, as is the evaluation of group performance. Hence, anyone who feels that social pressures prevent his doing or saying what he believes is right can use member-centered meetings to further his counterattack.

V: USES IN MULTILEVEL ORGANIZATIONS

19. NEW DEVELOPMENTS IN MANAGEMENT

For those who wish to go into the growth of participative management, we report briefly on two developments that are examples of the combination of vision and practicality which has characterized the revolution in the best of American industry during the past twenty-five years.

During the depression of the 1930's, a man named Joe Scanlon worked for a company which was saved from bankruptcy by a union committee that labored hand in glove with the company president to reduce costs. Scanlon was the spark plug of that committee. He later went to MIT and there developed what is known as the "Scanlon Plan," an outgrowth of the earlier joint labor-management effort.

One stimulating feature of the plan is that normally all members of the company, except possibly members of top management, receive each month a proportionate share of savings resulting from reductions in costs. The other is a method of participation that utilizes the know-how and ingenuity of every member. Under the plan, member-centered committees representing every group and function receive and evaluate every suggestion for reducing costs, and put into effect those considered workable.

"The psychological significance of this," says Douglas McGregor, "is that the Scanlon Plan 'fits together' the purposes of the organization with the natural human tendency to collaborate when collaboration is the sensible way to do things."[*]

Proponents of the plan cite a multitude of examples of increased

---

[*] "The Scanlon Plan Through a Psychologist's Eyes," in F. G. Lesieur, *The Scanlon Plan* (New York: John Wiley & Sons, Inc., 1958).

profits, higher productivity, lower costs, better working relationships, and even improved management.

What Dr. Rensis Likert calls "the newer theory of management" has grown from the studies made by the Survey Research Center of the University of Michigan, which he started in 1946. The Center has studied many large corporations and some large components of government. These studies have shown not only why the Scanlon Plan has had such good results but that the principle of participation works successfully even when not tied to a monetary incentive.

The Center has found that "the greater the amount of participation"—and Likert reports that the giving and sharing of information is an essential step in participation—"the greater tends to be the productivity of that unit and the greater the satisfaction of its members. An organization will function best when its personnel function not as individuals but as members of highly effective work groups with high performance goals. Consequently, management should deliberately build these effective groups, linking them into an overall organization by means of people who hold overlapping group membership. The superior in one group is a subordinate in the next group, and so on through the organization. If the work groups at each hierarchical level are well knit and effective, the linking process will be accomplished well."*

This newer theory of management, Likert thinks, combines the "best of job organization and the cooperative motivation system" and will go on to improve the combination further. His point of view—like that of Douglas McGregor in *The Human Side of Enterprise***—is shaped to the end of utilizing the human resources in an organization, which older patterns of management usually failed to do. His principles have developed from the finding of the social scientists that, though management pressure can run up an impressive record of production and earnings for the short run, it breeds hostility and eventual self-defeating trouble on the way. The participative form of management takes a bit longer to achieve more profitable records, but it holds them once obtained and generates further advance.

---

* This quotation and the illustration on page 123 are from Rensis Likert, *New Patterns of Management* (New York: McGraw-Hill, 1961).
** Douglas McGregor, *The Human Side of Enterprise* (New York: McGraw-Hill, 1960).

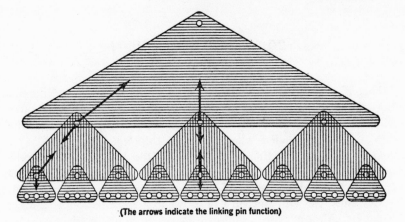

(The arrows indicate the linking pin function)

The Linking Pin

Executives accustomed to the authoritarian pattern on which practically all organizations are built may find this newer theory not even believable. Yet it has come from fifteen years of scientifically controlled analysis of what works best and worst in many large and successful companies and has been used effectively, sometimes in such surprising places as Army installations.

Since the Survey Research Center makes its studies on a confidential basis, the published reports do not name the client corporations, but articles summarizing the work and Likert's *New Patterns of Management* are full of supporting data. These include means for measuring the human elements in an organization and their effects on it. The behavioral scientists have worked out measures that enable management to assess the effects of management philosophy and supervisory behavior, and what Likert calls the "intervening variables": attitudes, expectations and motivations of supervisors and subordinates. Management can then relate these data to the more familiar criteria of production, costs, and earnings.

Member-centered meetings, as we mentioned earlier, are an essential part of participative management, but even when a company has not adopted that method, officials can use those meetings for a variety of purposes—as we suggest in the following chapters.

20. COMMUNICATION

" 'They'll' never realize," an employee once said, "the difference between what 'they' think we think, and what we think." And as things stand in the majority of organizations, it might be added that "we" don't often realize what "they" are thinking either.

Organizations put this problem under the heading of failure in communication, and panaceas turn up periodically to improve "getting the word down" or "up" or even "across" the line.

Certainly the full measure of truth and information is hard to come by. Almost every employee learns to sum up his supervisor with relative swiftness, and thereafter to shape and censor his words according to what he thinks the supervisor will want to hear. He doesn't feel he's being dishonest, merely circumspect. It is only sensible to sift the truth, and the more authoritarian his superior, the finer the mesh he uses to do so.

Thus at each mounting level of the organizational pinnacle, the man in charge is getting less of the truth as it is filtered through these self-preservative sieves, with the man at the top getting least of all. He turns to his immediate assistants for information and recommendations. But each of them sees the needs and difficulties from the angle of his department. Even supplementing with field trips—part of the "across" process—does not yield that full measure.

Alter the Relationship

The crux of the problem—this blocking or deflecting of information which should flow freely along the channels of communication —seems to be in the relationship of the superior to his subordinates. That relationship, therefore, became one of the starting points in the social scientists' research.

Their concern lay in trying to analyze and evaluate answers to the kinds of questions we put here very crudely. "How often do you have any contact with your superior? How much do you tell him about what's going on? Does telling him do any good? Does he listen to you and do anything about what you say? How often does he hold meetings? Is there any point in them or are they just talk? How free do you feel to talk about your problems with him? How free to set your own timetable for production? Does he think of you as a human being? Does he show any interest in you? Will he fight for you beyond this office or shop?" And so on, with, of course, other questions concerning their estimate of their superior and how they felt about working under him.

Very much telescoped and oversimplified, the gist of some of this key research can be given in two quotations from Dr. Likert:*

> Superiors at every level influence their subordinates' evaluation of them by the frequency with which they hold meetings [both formal and informal] and the extent to which they display interest in the ideas of their subordinates and make use of those ideas.

> The greater the superior's skill in using group methods of supervision, the greater are the productivity and the job satisfaction of his subordinates.

From these findings certain changes in the existing organization pattern seemed called for, to set in motion improvements in motivation and performance. Long-time pilot tests are now under way to find whether or not these changes will make a significant difference in these factors. In the meantime the social scientists made immediate tests of their validity. If the findings—welded into what Dr. Likert calls the "newer theory of management"—were valid, those departments and units of a company which came closest to exemplifying them should prove the most successful. And so, put to this empirical test, they did.

"It can be concluded, therefore," says Likert, "that management will make full use of the potential capacities of its human resources only when each person in an organization is a member of one or more effectively functioning work groups that have a high degree of group loyalty, effective skills of interaction and high performance goals."**

The "Highly Effective Group"

As Likert points out and anybody can testify, groups can work well or badly, and for either good or bad ends. There is no magic in a group, per se. Nor is there magic in just holding frequent meet-

---

* Op. cit., pp. 26–27.
** Ibid., p. 27.

ings unless the members feel that the superior is listening to what they are saying and will act on it.

A group, indeed, will only become a highly effective one when its leader and members have learned to have a supportive relationship to one another, and have learned such group skills as those outlined in Chapter 13.

The authoritarian superiors, who can only operate by keeping their subordinates dependent, obviously cannot take on this new role. Others, who hesitate and are uncertain of how they will adjust to it, can make use of the human-relations training now available. It is being given by trainers skilled in doing so, either from the outside or, in an increasing number of organizations, the inside.

But even without this training, the ground rules of member-centered meetings are such that they can help those superiors willing to make the effort to establish a participative relationship with their work groups. (As has been said, subordinates don't want to have "a sense of participation"; they want to participate.) The superiors are by all odds the right people to lead such meetings with their work groups. The fringe benefits by way of improved morale are great when those ordinarily in the commanding spot are able to create an atmosphere in which discussion is free. The superiors will also learn much about their own behavior, for in a participative group people will say what they would never say to an authoritarian boss.

Where Does Management Begin?

Whether the question is one of reorganizing on the basis of over-lapping work groups, or changing the climate and atmosphere of management, it is agreed that the ideal would be for the change to be instigated by the top man and begin with the relationship between him and his assistants. In many cases this is being done.

Short of this ideal, the sensible move seems to be to begin on a pilot or step-by-step basis. A gradual changeover to participation may also contribute to its greater success. Research* has confirmed what an observant person suspects: when a tight control is too suddenly lifted, the people thus released may turn on their releasers, or refuse to trust their new freedom, or abuse it or react in a variety

---

* R. K. White and R. O. Lippitt, *Autocracy and Democracy* (New York: Harper, 1960).

of seemingly ungrateful ways. This comes as an unpleasant surprise to those concerned, and if not anticipated, can convince them that the projected participation was a mistake.

Here are possible starting points from which member-centered meetings could be helpful in getting—and giving—a greater measure of true information.

A Suggestion for the Suggestion Box

One method for bridging the gap between "we" and "they," which many managements have tried with varying degrees of success, is that of the suggestion box. Their aim has been to induce officials and employees at all levels to contribute their ideas on how the organization's operations might be improved. Top-level officials make speeches, notices appear in house organs, placards are hung on walls and bulletin boards. All invite suggestions and mention awards for those accepted.

When the suggestions are supposed to be sent up the chain of command, they usually start trickling in slowly and never come in great volume or produce many useful ideas. This is not surprising. Most suggestions, if made, would point up or imply weaknesses in that chain of command. Sending them through it offers the potential suggester little hope and much danger.

When the system arranges for a suggester to send his ideas directly to a central staff of suggestion analysts, who will appraise it without knowing his identity, the initial response may be quite lively and provide some useful ideas. But what happens next is that the appraising group sends the best ideas back to the suborganization it would affect, for an evaluation. There they may often encounter inertia, fear, or hostility—"What fool thinks he can tell us how to do our job?" After some delay they are frequently rejected.

Rejected suggestions normally greatly exceed those accepted, and most rejections leave disappointed employees in their wake. Potential suggesters return to their former lethargy. Eventually top officials start a new campaign and the cycle is repeated. A lot of dust is stirred up and falls again.

Broaden the Base

Employees and lower level officials have plenty of suggestions to make. They also have plenty of complaints which are often tip-offs to needed improvements and therefore may lead to valuable suggestions. But the gulf between willing suggester (or complainer) and willing listener needs a better bridge than most suggestion systems provide. Under favorable conditions, member-centered meetings can provide the bridge.

The basic change needed from most existing systems is for management to solicit group rather than individual suggestions. Group suggestions have these advantages:

1. They give the suggesters anonymity and also discourage the employee who has many half-baked ideas and may be more interested in getting recognition than in producing a real improvement.

2. Groups produce fewer but better suggestions. Before submission the originating group does an appraising and sifting job, thinking through each idea, its implications, and the problem of applying it.

3. Developing suggestions improves cooperation among the group members, and when an award is made, the sharing of it avoids the jealousy which is often a by-product of individual awards. Also, a shared award encourages the members to try again.

4. A group suggestion gets a better hearing from both impartial reviewers and people whose work it would affect indirectly, because group suggestions usually are better thought out and their applicability is more easily recognized.

Possible Ways to Do It

A group suggestion plan can function successfully only if top management not only endorses but actively encourages and fosters it. Why this is so, anyone can see. Except for a real authoritarian, the usual superior can recognize and accept good ideas from his subordinates. What he does not like is for *his* superior to discover that the suggestion for improvement did not come from him, but from those whom he is supervising. "I should have thought of that," becomes "Because I didn't think of that, top management will think I'm no good at my job." His temptation is to reject the suggestion.

This is such an altogether human and general reaction that it is a difficult one to obviate. The Scanlon Plan met it early in its functioning, and Frederick G. Lesieur tells of its handling with such succinctness that his words are worth quoting. Nothing will be accomplished, he says, until "the company, and that is top management, convinces the foremen or the supervisors that they are being measured differently than in the past. If The Plan is to work the company will evaluate its lower management group on the basis that the best foreman or supervisor is the one whose department has the most suggestions. This means that this is a department where the people are not afraid to speak up. They are not afraid to participate and to say just how their job might be done easier and better. The old idea that the boss does all the thinking and the employees just do the work is dead."*

If a superior—backed by top management and his own immediate superior—gives his subordinates a positive go-ahead signal on holding group meetings of their own to devise suggestions for improvement, and convinces them of his honest and impartial judgment on the suggestions, that is a major step in itself. It is a declaration that he respects their judgment and wishes their participation in the functioning of the department.

If he can go further, offering to lead group suggestion meetings himself at regular or frequent intervals and conducting them in member-centered fashion, the gain in motivation and performance will be considerable. A pattern for participation will have been cut, which can act as a model for meetings held to discuss departmental problems and their solution. Many decisions the superior must make for himself, but those whose outcome will affect the whole group will benefit by having the shared concern and problem-solving efforts of the group.

Getting Information Down the Line

Not as many psychological blocks clog the passage of information going down as do those clogging the flow on the way up. Still, there remain the questions of whether the action will be carried out as the head office intended, and whether the individuals affected will give the changes more than grudging acceptance.

People dislike changing their habits. A major shift in policy or procedure usually forces them to do so. When that shift comes by fiat, without their having any share in the formulation, their failure

---

* Op. cit., p. 47.

to carry it out as intended is not always the result of misunderstanding alone.

They learn new policies from top-level speeches, house organs, and company leaflets. Directives are conveyed by regulations in a new manual of rules and procedures. These are helpful and usually necessary guide lines, but they are not a guarantee of appropriate performance.

Some executives get concurrence on preliminary drafts of a new directive from officials at lower levels, and the more concurrences obtained, the better the understanding and the subsequent results. This remains a slow and cumbersome process, one rarely able to elicit the concurrence of all the people whom the new directive will affect. But each person who will be affected by the changes needs desperately to know what will be expected of him. His boss will judge him by his performance. How will his particular job be changed? What, precisely, will be expected of him? Does the new directive mean that he goes on with what he's presently doing and some new duties too? Just what *does* it mean?

If—a most important if—decisions on how the details of a new policy or directive are to be implemented can be left up to the groups who will be doing the job, the subsequent results will be decidedly improved.

Real Concurrence

Let's assume the matter at issue is that of getting the desired action on a directive, and a member- or worker-centered meeting is held in every section or department whose functions it will affect. If the meeting can be held in a room having a blackboard within view of everyone, good. If not, the easel routine will have to suffice. Preferably all the workers in the room are provided with a copy of the new directive, which they may take up paragraph by paragraph or even sentence by sentence. What does this word mean, this phrase? Exactly how will it work? What new problems does this bring and how do we propose to handle them? How will this effect each function we perform? Will it work?

If the group is slow with questions or reluctant to put them, breaking it into buzz groups will expedite the queries. If a problem needs solving, those small, divided sessions will improve analysis at each step, also serving, as we mentioned before, to subdue and harness the energies of the griper and to remind the prima donna that he is not unique.

Some points in the directive may baffle understanding, although the workers who know their jobs can usually come up with the answers. If they can't, they and the leader-supervisor must decide whether to question the instruction or to assume the action it intended. Before they make that decision, they can thrash out the question of what harm or benefit their assumption will entail.

By the time the members have thus analyzed their future functions in relation to the directive (1) they have a pretty firm idea of their individual jobs in connection with it, (2) they feel involved in the results, (3) they have often cut across the usual networks and alliances endemic in any working situation, and (4) they have begun to work together as a group.

Short Cuts for the Analyst

The man who walks into a subgroup to "analyze its performance" with an eye to improving it is seldom welcomed by that unit's members. The reaction at the receiving end ranges from suspicion and distrust to irritation at the prospect of how much time they will have to spend answering his questions and producing for him the documents he will be sure to want. In some, his coming creates actual fear for their jobs. All of them consider him an intruder and there is an instinctive closing of the ranks against him.

Yet the studies he makes are important. The best evidence of this, if any is needed, is that the organizations doing the most to improve themselves are already very good. Some consider the analyses important enough to hire outside consultants to make them; others maintain analyst teams on their own staffs.

The analyst's task is to gather his facts, verify them, fit them together into a reasonable picture, and make recommendations which both he and his company hope the unit will be willing to act on with some degree of enthusiasm. Obviously almost every stage of this process depends on the cooperation of the key people in the unit who—along with everyone else in it—resent his coming.

A member-centered meeting with those key people at the start of the survey and another later, if distrust lingers or is reawakened, can help break down resistance and act as a short cut to fact-finding and verifying. More such meetings might be useful, but few units would be able to spare the time.

That first meeting is opened by the proper authority in the unit, who then leaves if both he and the analyst have agreed that discussion will be freer without him. (If he is accustomed to meet with his men on a free-discussion basis, his presence will be a great help.) The analyst then goes ahead to say precisely and with total honesty why he is there. He puts every card he can think of on the table, so nothing is held in reserve. He further corroborates the openness of his intentions by distributing copies of a statement he has written outlining the purposes of the study. Once the participants have read that, he tells them he has asked for this meeting so they will have a chance to question and discuss the statement with him.

He invites questions and, if the response is not immediate, waits briefly and reiterates his request in slightly different words. Then, if the participants are still reluctant to ask, or the questions seem to be coming too slowly, he breaks them into buzz groups, asking them to spend ten minutes developing questions. When these come, he explores every one with the members to be sure they have a common understanding of it and then enlists their comments. Frequently he finds that the original question provokes more, some of which may give him leads on problems in the unit. When the group has clarified a question, the analyst gives the answer.

One important point is the freedom of the discussion. To create the climate for this, the analyst does not direct their talk, but keeps the discussion on the subject, clarifies dubious points, clears up misimpressions, and makes certain that all viewpoints are explored. The other essential point is the honesty of his answers. This is the key to his winning the unit's confidence.

After all the questions about the survey's purpose have been answered, the participants are far more ready to tell the analyst what things they think he will need to learn about their work and how they would go about finding them, were they in his shoes. His part, again, is that of asking and listening, never criticizing anything said by a member of the group but asking him to clarify it when necessary.

After that initial meeting, of course, the analyst has to concern himself primarily with getting facts from individuals. Like his coming in the first place, these separate sessions may be a divisive factor, reactivating the latent uneasiness of the unit. Should he sense this, he can request time for another member-centered meeting, at which he explains his need for help on certain specified problems. He admits he is stuck at such and such a point for lack of information. Then he goes on with, "Now when this situation occurs, precisely what happens?" What the members see as problems—not to mention a new understanding by them of their colleagues' problems— usually emerges from such a session. Buzz sessions can be resorted to again, if necessary. This second meeting also serves to verify the facts collected in the interviews.

Besides their psychological usefulness, the meetings will:

1. Lessen the preliminary and fact-finding time.
2. Give the analyst a short cut to the unit members' good ideas.
3. Provide a quick test for the practicality of the analyst's ideas.
4. Give the members the background needed to understand the analyst's subsequent recommendations.
5. Contribute to a better reception of those recommendations because people will do much more to make a solution work when they have had a share in developing it.

21. SITUATIONS WITH BUILT-IN TROUBLE

Almost any kind of dividing line between parts of an organization is likely to be bordered on both sides by resentments that usually just smolder away without doing too much harm, like fires in a peat bog. But given a half plausible excuse, they flare up into real conflict.

People in the field, for instance, think those in the main office "simply don't understand our problems out here." People in the head office think those in the field are caught up in their own small turmoil and fail to see problems in perspective. The inevitable reaction is for each side to blame the other and each often does a bit of foot dragging when a disagreement occurs.

To show further uses of member-centered meetings, we've picked two other omnipresent examples from the many situations where a dividing line creates these resentments and conflicts.

Line-Staff Resentments

Almost every multilevel organization is built around what the military call the chain of command. This is a descending series of bosses, each of whom is responsible for doing the job assigned to his level and seeing that his subordinates, in turn, do theirs at their level.

The resentments arise because there is also a shadow chain of command, with a second series of bosses, and often the result is two conflicting ideas of what (or how) things should be done. These two chains are called Line and Staff. Line workers make, handle, and sell the products; Staff workers are occupied with research and planning, or with various supporting services such as budgeting, accounting, and maintenance.

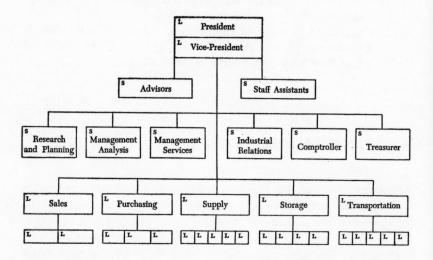

Each Staff man becomes a specialist in his field. If he works at an upper level, he prepares instructions on how the plans he prepares and the boss approves are to be carried out, how the accounts are to be kept, or maintenance performed. At whatever level he is, part of his job is to see that Line people follow these instructions effectively.

Line workers, for their part, are concerned with producing and handling and shipping. But they have to do these jobs, alas, in the ways prescribed by Staff. They would be less than human if they didn't think Staff workers were visionaries who didn't know how to put their minds to practical problems.

Staff workers—again, alas—are sometimes inclined to push their authority too far, often with the implication that they, after all, "see the boss every day and know what he wants."

Conflicts across this dividing line are endemic. Either side enjoys catching the other out and is not above an effort—presumably an unconscious one—to do so. Resentments no longer remain in the smoldering stage.

There are also misunderstandings, which may be simply that, and nothing more ominous. There is the classic example of an Army official who complained that he sent trucks to the shop for repairs which should take two days of work and cost about fifteen dollars per truck, but they came back to him months later with bills for five hundred dollars each. What happened was that the repair manual (Staff-prepared) said that trucks must be made operational. To the official who sent the trucks for repair, a truck was "operational" if it would run; to the man running the repair shop, it was "operational" only when he had made it as good as new.

Volunteer and Paid Workers

It doesn't require special diagnostic skill to spot the probable source of resentment in any situation where some people give their time to the success of an organization and others are paid for theirs. In the large associations and clubs supported by public donations or the dues of the members, a paid staff is essential.

The resentment here is found most often at the top level, where policy-making volunteers and paid professional staff come together. The volunteers are eager to get the job done and are impatient with the minutiae of its accomplishment. The staff, on the other hand, has a professional stake in how it is done. "They spill the gravy," said one paid staff member, "and we have to clean it up."

Occasionally a volunteer recognizes his lack of technical schooling and is amiably willing to be advised by a staff member. More frequently the volunteer is a competent person in his own right, and the paid staff member is deprived of even the small comfort of feeling superior. He has no recourse but to be quiet and—in an unacknowledged way—subservient. He may have done all the research; he is responsible for all the needed documents; he may be bursting with solutions for sticky problems. But when the board or the committee meets, it is his place not to speak unless spoken to. Often he does not get, or get clearly, guidance he badly needs to do a job the Board wants.

Cut Across the Line

When the conflicts arise, as they usually do where these dividing lines exist, a member-centered meeting, or a series of them, can help the impatient volunteers and frustrated professionals put their problems back into perspective.

If a meeting starts with a census of common operating problems (it would be fatal to begin with one-side-of-the-line problems) and the discussion is carried on in member-centered fashion, each side will get glimpses of the difficulties faced by the other. A lessening of antipathies should follow. It is even possible for enough breaks to be made in the dividing line so it will never again be solid.

The meetings will have accomplished a considerable amount if they help the members realize that it is the dividing line itself which is the target of their resentment—not necessarily the people working on either side.

Coordinating Proposed Changes

The vertical dividing line is not the only built-in source of trouble. The following sticking point in organization procedures, at one stage of which member-centered meetings can be helpful, results from the fragmentation inevitable in a large organization. Pieces of a difficulty are scattered in various sections. One of the hardest jobs of the over-all management is to make sure that the successful solution of a problem in one suborganization will not cause worse problems in another.

The need is to tie all the pieces together, and to accomplish this, more or less the following procedure takes place.

"Topside" requests the management analysis staff to study a particular difficulty, come up with a solution, and see to it that all divisions affected will also benefit from the solution. It is the last chore that is the hardest.

A—standing for a single man or a team of men—goes to each

of the divisions to analyze its share of the difficulty. He gets suggestions, analyzes them, considers them in the light of his own ideas, and selects the proposals which seem to tie together. He works them into a coherent plan. He takes that plan to his superior and makes the changes in it which his superior demands and can't be talked out of. He then dispatches it to the proper people in the other divisions "for comment." Let us say these other divisions are Budget, Finance, and Planning.

The recipient of the plan in Budget raises objections, thinks up counterproposals, and takes the plan—increased by *his* amendments —to his superior for approval. That approval obtained, he returns the document to A. By now the Budget men have the vested interest in their changes that an act of creation, however small, always entails. In the meantime Finance and Planning have gone through like performances and are also feeling possessive about their amendments.

A now has his plan back on his hands, so bristling with "comments" that he finds it scarcely recognizable. For him lies ahead the tedious and often infuriating task of resolving all the conflicts— not to mention obtaining final approval of the various superiors to the solutions.

Traditional meetings bringing together all involved in the plan are often tried at this stage. They are an obvious short cut. Before them A has done his own resolving of the comments, gotten his superior's concurrence, and distributed the results to those involved. When the meeting takes place, A is entrenched in his position, very much on the defensive and eager to counterattack. So are Budget, Finance, and Planning. Considerable infighting follows, usually resulting in compromises which come nowhere near solving the problem. A concludes that in the future he will approach one person after another over the lunch table or on the telephone.

A can use a member-centered meeting, or a series of them, with a good chance of success at this stage if he has schooled himself to be a catalytic leader working for a constructive solution that all divisions will cooperate in carrying out. As such, he doesn't take sides. He listens while certain members are letting off steam, trying to sift out the prejudices and fit the facts together. He summarizes, makes notes on the blackboard, and moves the meeting along by asking questions such as, "What are we really disagreeing about?" and

"How would that work in the other divisions?" Through this and other approaches (see Chapter 16) the group may progress toward an integrated solution.

Several such meetings may be required, but a final "for your concurrence" memo at the end can be a mere formality. The members are only concurring in a solution they helped to bring about.

22. SELECTING PERSONNEL

One of the newer ways being used to judge applicants for a job, or candidates for promotion, is a group oral interview. It is like a member-centered meeting in that the candidates themselves are responsible for the course of the discussion, and the principle on which it works is that people handle themselves differently in a group and reveal different qualities from those appearing in a private interview.

Five or six candidates who have already successfully skimmed over the hurdles set up by the Personnel Department sit around a table, their names on placards in front of them. Examiners sit with them, wordlessly listening and reaching their separate conclusions about the qualities of the candidates as they carry on the discussion.

Each candidate is given a typed account of a problem or a topic, and the whole group is told to talk about it. They have had no chance to prepare, and they have no clue to the subject until they are faced with the need to summon all their capabilities in the effort to discuss it. What happens is that they soon forget they are being observed and, as Jules Willing* said in writing about such an interview, "The most illuminating part of this technique is the way poses begin to crumble and genuine personality shows through."

Obviously such a group interview is only worth the investment

* See "Personnel," *American Management Association,* Vol. 39, #2, March-April, 1962.

in time and money when the waiting jobs call for the kinds of skills it will reveal: quick, clear thinking and the ability to handle oneself well in what is essentially a group situation. It has great value when the positions to be filled are executive ones, or are based on working with people or meeting the public. Some people become shy or tongue-tied in a group; others can come up with excellent solutions for a problem but they have to go slowly, or work by themselves. Still others talk badly but write well. For such as these, or for those whose interests lie in scientific research, a group interview can save much subsequent futile effort, and suggest to the personnel department that these people be considered for more appropriate jobs.

The interviews can be used to meet the requirements of varying situations by tailoring the questions provided. The following is how such interviews are used to pick potential executives.

For Executive Positions

The interviewees sit around or on both sides of a table, with one examiner at each end. They are told what the procedure is to be, handed the typed statement of a problem, given a brief time to digest it, and then instructed to discuss how they would go about solving it. The first discussion is usually cut off in twenty-five to thirty minutes—sooner if the examiners feel it is lagging—and then another problem is handed around for discussion, and still another if the examiners would like further observation. The over-all time should be held to an hour and a half.

Setting the Problem for Discussion

It usually falls to the lot of the personnel department—in collaboration with the potential bosses or superiors concerned—to prepare the problems to be discussed. Several are prepared in advance, fifteen or twenty if possible, having these over-all specifications:

1. They should be set or selected after reviewing the records of the various candidates to be interviewed, to avoid immediately touching the background of any one candidate, which would, of course, give him a special advantage.
2. They should avoid technical problems and language unless the job or promotion lies in a highly technical field.

3. They should have emotional content and be capable of sparking controversy. They can reflect a news item or an operational difficulty in the candidates' experience. Good ones come from actual episodes in a pertinent department of the organization. The ideal is one which so captures the group's interest that its audience is forgotten.
4. They should provide a reasonable basis for argument on either side, preferably posing the kind of problem about which people say, "I really don't know *what* I would do in that case." But they should not touch on racial, religious, or political beliefs.

Examples of Problems

This problem was used with young people who were fresh from an academic background.

In a certain college the student newspaper is printed in the college printing shop and has a wide paid circulation among alumni. The editorial board is made up of students elected by the student body as their representatives. Recently the editorial columns of the paper have been devoted to repeated, outspoken attacks on the policies of the college administration. The administration has carefully examined the policies in question and has decided they are essential to maintain. The reasons for this decision have been discussed with student leaders who have, however, rejected those reasons as invalid. The college administration has begun to receive from alumni protests obviously inspired by the editorials. Proposals have been made that various sanctions be invoked against the paper, ranging from actual suspension of publication to withdrawing the privilege of having it printed by college facilities. You are a committee of faculty and administration who have met to discuss what action to take in this situation. What are your recommendations?

The next problem reveals attitudes irrespective of age or working experience.

A certain individual has been arrested several times for unprovoked assaults of extreme brutality. Psychiatrists declare he is not legally insane, but that his mental and emotional make-up are such that he can be expected to continue his career of violence. There is no legal provision in the jurisdiction in question for compulsory hospitalization of anyone who is not certifiably insane. He has just finished serving his most recent jail sentence. The police keep an eye on him and, to keep him out of circulation, arrest him on any pretext. His lawyer terms this "persecution" and also resists efforts to send the man to a mental hospital on a voluntary basis. You are a committee of citizens gathered together voluntarily to see what can be done to safeguard the community.

The third might be taken as a sample of those plucked from the memory or files of an executive. This could be used for a group in line for promotion.

You are the manager of an assembly plant, and a long-distance call from the company's headquarters has just told you that your plant and several others are to be closed in six months, the end of your busiest season. The work will be transferred to a new plant several hundred miles away, which you are to manage. What problems do you anticipate? What do you plan to do about them?

The role of the examiners is purely that of listening, observing, and making notes, while the discussion is going on. They should be unknown to the candidates, but the candidates are already known to them on paper, in the summaries and documents supplied them by the personnel office. Of course they must have no personal stake in the selections.

When the discussion session has finished, the examiners talk to some candidates separately, to fill gaps in their impressions or to test conclusions reached during the session. Then they begin their homework. Each prepares a report on each candidate, using a form developed by the personnel department for those potential jobs or promotions.

Questions like the following have been used as criteria for college graduates being considered as potential executives.

1. *Personality*

   Did you like him? Did he have poise? How was his grammar? Did he speak easily? Did the others listen to him? Could you detect qualities—good or bad—which would have a significant effect on other people? Was he overbearing? Did a resonant voice and confident manner make his ideas seem better than they were?

2. *Approach to Solving the Problem*

   Could he isolate the basic issues? Did he successfully apply his own knowledge or experience to solving the problem? Did he bring up material that was relevant? Or trivia?

3. *Creativity*

Did he originate solutions or ideas? If so, did they hold up under group examination? Did he develop ideas, once presented? Did he jump in too fast, with too many ideas, some useless? If so, do you think experience on a job would discipline his thinking, or is he the type who will always speak impulsively?

4. *Practicality*

Did he talk only about theories or did he show—regardless of how little practical experience he has had—some awareness of the practical difficulties involved in suggested solutions?

5. *Evidences of Leadership—Intellectual*

Was he helpful in putting the problem in some kind of perspective? Did he suggest ways of doing so to others? Did he summarize successfully? Help move the discussion toward a solution?

6. *Evidences of Leadership—Ability to Work with a Group*

Did he help create a sense of naturalness in the group? Help members work together? Did he show appropriate confidence in himself and his ideas? Did he let others contribute? Did he show appreciation for the good ideas of others? How did he react when his own ideas were rejected by them? When he was interrupted by them? When other peoples' ideas were beside the point did he get the discussion back on the subject? Without irritating the others?

The examiners can only base their judgments on what they perceive, but that proves to be a surprising amount, and rarely conflicting. When they talk together after the session they find also that they serve as a check on each other's prejudices.

Then they write up their individual reports, referring not only to their personal impressions, but to any contradictions they find between those impressions and evidence supplied them by the personnel department on the candidates. Each examiner's verdicts run "Yes," "No," or "Maybe"—the last category meaning that the candidate might do adequately in some other field which the examiner suggests. When he gives the verdict "No," he gives the specific reasons for his decision.

Variation on the Pattern

One company has found its "round-table interview" a great time-saving device in selecting young people for training, and one which has resulted in better selections. Because the possible candidates were seen together, in discussion, the executives who needed to look them over did not have to go through the repetitive and often wearying process of one separate interview after another.

In the procedure reported by Mr. Willing,* an interview leader sits with the candidates and explains the forthcoming session. He hands them topics, not problems, and they are expected to talk only ten to fifteen minutes on each topic. Then the executives who are to judge the qualities of the young people come into the room and take their places outside the circle. They are not introduced; they change their places after the discussion of each topic "in order to neutralize any personal interaction between them and the candidates," and they say nothing. In addition to a rating sheet, each executive has with him a brief summary of the backgrounds of the candidates.

Because Mr. Willing's company is looking for three separate sets of characteristics—selling, engineering, and manufacturing abilities—the topics are slanted toward subjects which would elicit evidence of the wanted characteristics.

Along with his comment on how "poses crumble" in the group discussions, Mr. Willing says of his experience, "One learns a lot about how people disagree with each other!"

23. TRAINING PERSONNEL

The first real nine-to-five job one of us had was in a bookstore, and nothing that took place in its three large rooms could have been classified as formal training. Instead, the new employee was handed art gum and a dust rag, and put to the job of cleaning every book

---

* Ibid.

in the place. The words that accompanied the dust rag were, "If you take a book off the shelf, clean it, and *handle* it, you will never forget where it is. You will be able to locate it instantly for any customer." This was training by doing in its most primitive form. But it worked, as the method always does, better than indoctrination alone.

Over the last twenty years training courses for new employees and booster courses for experienced ones have come much closer to the principle of "handling the book." Case studies have been introduced; lectures are now accompanied by a variety of visual aids, and often the employee is given some actual experience of the kind of situation he will encounter on the job. But much of it still remains a generalized indoctrination, and it is the rare employee who ever looks again at the notes he took on the fifty-minute speeches covering "what we do in our department." It is possible that he will remember the charts and columns of figures—blown up to be visible from the back of the room—but we doubt it. (We also doubt that he can ever again hear the words "work as a team" without wincing.)

What he is likely to remember is what he learned from working through actual problems of immediate or future concern to him. And if at every stage of that work the obstacles he runs into form the nucleus of problem-solving sessions, free discussions, buzz sessions, and role-playing if necessary, the impact will be still greater. The instructor's point is to involve him personally, throwing to him as much responsibility as he can take. The instructor is less concerned with the learner's coming up with a correct solution than with his achieving a how-to-go-about-it skill. Accuracy will come with experience on the job and correction by his superior.

A problem-centered training session, with the responsibility for solutions directed to the trainee, does not require more time in the execution than do more traditional ones. It does, however, require more advance thinking on the part of the instructor. The chores of requesting speakers and riding herd on the reproduction department for slides and blown-up charts are gone. What replaces them are major efforts of his imagination.

He must determine his goals and the materials to be covered just as precisely as he would for a more traditional course, at the same time allowing flexibility in his plan so he can adapt it to utilize problems the trainees themselves will present. He has to pinpoint actual problems of immediate concern to the learners and try to estimate the time required for their solution. This includes anticipating obstacles ahead for the trainees and gauging how many hours of analysis and discussion will be needed to reduce them. The instructor must at each stage try to project himself into the minds of those who have not yet begun to accumulate relevant experience.

The instructor should also have had experience in leading member-centered meetings, so he knows the uses and limitations of buzz sessions, the virtues of the blackboard in problem solving, when role-playing will help and when it will prove only a pleasant diversion—and above all how to be a catalyst.

Examples of Training Situations

We have outlined below suggested plans as worked out in three varying situations. The first and third are for trainees new to a job; the second can be adapted either to employees being trained for new work or to those getting training to improve their performance of old duties.

Training Course for Management Analysts

The training here involved work with men selected from various departments to provide them with the basic skills needed for management analysis work. The instructor used the summaries given under points 1 through 4 on pages 146–47 to express the factors essential to the training. The opening phase—held to a minimum—covered the tasks of general management and the nature of management analysis work. The next session was one of free discussion and buzz sessions. The trainees presented queries that had come to their minds in their course of reading, and when one appeared that lent itself as an example of the steps in problem solving, the instructor listed those steps on the blackboard in abbreviated form. He then led a step-by-step analysis of that problem and by the end of the day the group had an acceptable solution.

The instructor followed the five-step technique shown in point 3 on page 146 (example, reading, discussion, practice and evaluation) throughout. As the major part of the training, the group made an

Management Analysis Training Course

1. Purpose

To instill in each participant, to the extent of his ability, the skills used by a management analyst, so the participant can return to his department able to plan and conduct an initial management analysis with guidance from the training officer, and subsequent analyses with decreasing guidance.

2. Basic knowledge involved

The participants learn what the tasks of management are, the general nature of management-analysis work, and the relationship between the two. They also learn certain principles of leadership and communication which psychological research during recent years has isolated and made available.

3. Training principle

A skill can be learned only by practice, as an infant learns to walk, a child to ride a bicycle or play a game. The participants in the course learn each management analysis skill by a six-stage process. During the course they:

1. Learn about each skill through an instructor-led group performance of a simple example.
2. Read articles explaining the essentials of the skill.
3. Clarify the reading through discussion with the other participants and the instructor.

4. Practice the skill individually or in pairs, each man or pair examining different operations of the office being studied.

5. Jointly review the results of all the participants' use of the skill in Step 4. In doing this they determine what recommendations to make as a result of that part of the study and improve their understanding of the skill, the purposes for which it is useful, and how to use it effectively. Buzz sessions and role playing are important in these reviews.

After the course, comes Step 6, in which each participant uses what he has learned and improves his skills by performing his first projects in his own department under the training officer's guidance and by consulting as frequently as he wishes with other course members.

4. Skills acquired

Through the process outlined above, the participants acquire the skills needed to:

1. Solve problems through an orderly process.
2. Prepare and use a management analysis study plan.
3. Analyze an office procedure and flow of work.
4. Analyze the functions, structure, and working relationships of an organization.
5. Compare the costs of different ways of doing a job.
6. Measure workers' activity, production, or errors by counting.
7. Measure workers' activity, production, or errors by sampling.
8. Design a form.
9. Plan delegation and decentralization of authority.
10. Reduce resistance to change.
11. Present ideas.
12. Prepare a management analysis report.

actual methods-and-procedures survey. They started by jointly analyzing the plan of a previous survey. That afternoon each member studied printed material on planning a survey and the following day they jointly produced a plan for the one they were to make. On subsequent days they carried out their plan, learning a different technique of analysis at each step and developing suggested improvements from the use of each. The training also had a useful by-product. The trainees produced eighteen suggestions for improving the procedure and seventeen of them were adopted.

Improving Existing Performances

Though training courses are usually thought of as preparation for a new job, they are also important whenever people in various parts of an enterprise must learn new concepts.

When an important official becomes aware of a serious problem— a drop in sales or a delay in production, a serious failure in quality or a rise in costs—he tries first to pinpoint the source of the difficulty and then to work out a cure. That cure may be purely mechanical, but it is likely to involve people who need to be given a fresh impetus and more solid understanding of what they are doing.

For example, let's assume that the chosen solution for a company's hypothetical problem is an improved budget system. This would seem to be a goal unlikely to be accomplished through member-centered meetings. It is largely a mathematical process, one of organizing data to aid in making and carrying out decisions. Surely straight instruction should be enough.

Mathematical process though it is, budgeting does not exist in a vacuum. People decide what data are needed and which can be feasibly collected. The same ones devise the system for doing the collecting. Another set of people prepares the documents; a third has to analyze and evaluate the data, even if already summarized by electronic computers. Then the budget has to be put together and successfully presented. Imagination, understanding of people, and understanding of the company will have all to be brought into the process.

The general pattern for training given here can be cut, enlarged, or adapted, depending on whether the trainees are having a booster course to improve their existing performance or are being introduced to budget making. Newcomers would probably not be involved in all the following phases, but even if they are only to be at the bottom of the budget department totem pole, they'll benefit from the insight this type of training can give them.

This starting phase of the course outlined below is mainly for newcomers to budgeting. If a similar phase is planned for those already in the department, the reading and indoctrination are adapted to their needs.

In the initial days of the course some indoctrination has to take place on the nature and principles of budgeting, the particular system used in the organization, and how it relates to programing, accounting, and reporting. There is also an outline of over-all steps in developing and preparing a budget, and discussion of revisions that have taken place in recent years when the board of directors or legislature sliced off large amounts.

All this is general background information. Even so, the more of it that can be conveyed visually and with free discussion following, the better. Some people's threshold to boredom is lower than others—better plan the session with the lowest in mind.

With these necessary preliminaries out of the way the new trainees, or the partly experienced ones, are now put to the task of actually preparing a budget. Whenever he can, the leader-instructor bases the free discussions, the buzz sessions, the role-playing, on problems the trainees themselves bring up. Particularly if the trainees have already had some experience and are there to improve their performance, they will produce problems, examples, snags, and conflicts.

The leader has compiled the material with which they work: duplications of a set of figures submitted by various departments in some previous year—say 1963. At the same time he gives them the actual expenditures of the year 1962. Thus they work from the hopes of 1963 back to the realities of 1962, looking suspiciously at whatever seems out of line in the 1963 submissions. Each must then decide where the priorities for 1964 should lie, where cuts should be made, and where, less often, increases are in order to help carry out a change in policy or tactics. They then compare and discuss their individual estimates, using all the tools devised for a member-centered meeting to understand the impact of their tentative decisions, until they reach a consensus.

This setting of priorities for some departments and cuts for others is, as the experienced know, merely a declaration of war. To furnish the participants with some foretaste of how to conduct themselves during that war, so that though they emerge battle-scarred they can at least have won a negotiated victory, the leader has the trainees role-play.

Bill Young is dubbed chief of personnel and given personnel department's 25 per cent cut with the words, "You are completely immersed in the problems of your department. You don't think, you *know*, that the needs of no other department are equally important. You're going to get your request restored to the last dollar."

Ralph Blanchard, on the other hand, is briefed to hold the line against all but the most superconvincing factual evidence. He is to ring variation after variation on the query, "Why so much more this year than last when your program calls for no great change?" Each probes, reasons, argues, as he tears the submission apart item by item—without infuriating the other any more than is inevitable.

Once the role-playing has ended, the trainees can go into buzz sessions to go over how they think Blanchard handled himself, and to see if he might have lessened Young's anguish at some point. They also discuss whether Blanchard chose the proper items in the submissions to query. They perhaps thought other items the dubious ones. They go on to points Young might have made convincing but ignored or did not present well. If a resulting disagreement is sharp and important, a problem-solving session on that matter can be set up for the next meeting.

Several trainees can join the role-playing later when Young or Blanchard or any of the others has to justify the prepared budget to a mock finance or legislative committee.

One or more of the prepared forms used in this process may seem cumbersome or inadequate to the trainees as they work with them. If so, they may be able to find ways to improve them. This would be an important gain, and the changes they suggest could be discussed at once, put through the problem-solving wringer, and subjected to any mock experience-testing the group can devise.

The learning in depth that such a training experience can provide has an additional benefit for those in the group who have been working on their jobs for some time: they come through it with a new kind of rapport and working relationship, plus a better understanding of some of the problems faced by the different departments.

Training Session at Monze

The following training session is a far cry from that devoted to producing a budget in a multilevel organization—both geographically and in the content of the course. It is included to show the flexibility of the attitudes and methods used in training through member-centered meetings.

About a year before the Africans in Northern Rhodesia attained power in their government, one of the authors put on a short training course for seventeen Africans in that country who were about to be sent into villages by the government as community development assistants. Their future job was to stimulate the villagers to community action, whether the project they wanted was building a village school, a needed bridge, or a new well. Few of the participants had more schooling than the equivalent of our fifth grade. (Education is very hard for an African to obtain.) Accompanying the whole session was the African eagerness for independence from European (the usual term for "white") government and skepticism of anything stemming from that government.

The first step was to ask the trainees to form buzz groups and decide the most formidable difficulties they expected to meet in carrying out their jobs. In ten heated minutes of discussion the following emerged from their years of village living and were put on the blackboard:

Suspicion.

People don't follow what they're taught.

Dislike of previous government people.

Political tension and influence.

Wrong approach by community development assistants.

Ignorance.

Frequent changes of staff.

What the village wants conflicts with what the assistant thinks it needs.

Conflicting guidance from the assistant's superiors.

A few minutes of general discussion followed, to the end that "Wrong approach by the assistant" was identified as the difficulty of paramount concern. Another buzz session produced the unanimous conclusion that a "right" approach is one which enlists the support and participation of the influential people in any village.

But how to gain that support? Unanimity remained, but it was now unanimous perplexity. Then came the following interchange:

TRAINER: Who are the influential people?

ANSWERS: The chief, the headman, the politician, the storekeeper, the schoolmaster.

TRAINER: Are there some whose support is most needed, or most difficult to get?

ANSWERS: Sometimes the chief, sometimes the politician—usually the politician.

At this point the trainer had to find a way to clarify and resolve the very human conflict brought out by the discussion: that between the ranking politician of the village and the community development assistant whom the politician saw as a threat. He decided to use role-playing and worked into it this way:

TRAINER: That politician seems very much on your minds. What does he do?

ANSWERS: He's trying to strengthen_____or_____ (naming the two rival African political parties).

TRAINER: Would two of you be willing to act out what sometimes happens when a community development assistant approaches a politician? Who wants to be the politician? _____ Now. Who's willing to play the Assistant? _____ Okay, where are you going to have this talk take place?

ANSWERS: In the politician's hut.

TRAINER: What time of day?

ANSWERS: Maybe late afternoon.

TRAINER: All right. Now, politician, what are you doing when the assistant comes in?

ANSWER: Drinking beer.

TRAINER: Is that right, everybody? (They found it definitely right.) Okay, if you're ready, let's start.

The role players threw themselves into their parts with an enthusiasm any seasoned actor might have envied. The politician in particular relished his assignment, shifting from one defensive point to another, drawing recognition and laughter from his audience with each shift. The student playing the community development assistant also tried several lines of approach, but though he too drew appreciative laughter from his audience, he made no progress toward persuading the politician.

After a few minutes, a second pair tried its skill, then a third. The role-playing was then cut off, and the buzz groups were asked to reassemble to list all the excuses and points of resistance the three politicians had used. They proved to be:

He was against anything the present European-controlled government supported.

He wanted to postpone action until his party came to power.

He thought the community development assistant a government spy.

He feared the loss of his own prestige.

He did not want other villagers to advance.

He thought the assistant was afraid to show which political party he favored.

He was suspicious of the assistant's coming at this time.

He claimed the people were too poor to help with a community development project.

He misunderstood, either thinking community development was confined to certain areas, or that a project would take people to work in town, which he opposed.

Once the students saw those reactions listed on the blackboard, they had little hesitation in deciding that the most serious was the politician's thinking the assistant a spy, and their most important goal was the dispelling of that suspicion.

Buzz groups served again, this time to break the problem into analyzable portions. Discussions based on the question, "What kinds of activities would a politician expect of a spy?" produced eight answers, of which five were admitted to be activities also necessary to the assistants' own jobs. Each of these five activities was then explored separately, to see how an assistant could find a way to carry it out without inviting the suspicion of spying.

That session was the beginning of a week of demonstrations and practice. As the days passed, the community development assistants went on to explore other common problems and to develop joint answers from their own experiences. The center's training director, who had been observing the sessions, then tried his hand at running an exploratory session, and two of the trainees did the same. Each session produced information, attitudes, and problems previously unsuspected by the European staff in spite of many years of service, and the assistants reached solutions which gave them new insights.

The author's part in this whole project was limited to the two weeks' training outlined above, during which he also trained the permanent training director, a European, in the use of the techniques and approach of member-centered meetings. These, according to word received from him many months later, have become "the very core of the training at Monze." He went on:

> Even when I have to give a short talk on a particular subject, I invariably turn it into a group session. It is a wonderful way of getting to know what the trainees are thinking, it helps each one of them to make his or her contribution which can be shared by the class. But I think the most important contribution it has made to the training at Monze is the fact that it has given the trainees self-confidence.
>
> I may be wrong, but I think when you were at Monze we both felt that group work's main job was to help the trainees solve problems. With this I would agree, but after using it for over a year in my training programs, I feel it has done much more than this. What it has done for my trainees is to give them self-confidence. It has given them the ability to listen to other points of view, and it has taught them that other folk, however simple they may appear to be, have a contribution to make.

APPENDIX I

AIDS

Sample Structure and Content for a Recorder's Record

Subject	*Content*
What is Vic's problem?	Vic explains he has three sections under him; two of them depend on each other, but don't work with third group. Chief of third group the sticker—keeps all three working separately. What can Vic do?
Facts and Obstacles	Each section head loyal, competent. But each section like separate kingdom, loyal to its head. Needs to switch functions, but that one woman resists any change in her job. She's good at her job if she'd only cooperate better. She's the one who's holding everything up. Thinks she'd lose prestige. She's been told to switch functions and that it would be better for everybody. Obeys on surface, but hangs onto all details; won't let them go. Has Vic tried talking with her about it? All she does is get angry; keeps saying there must be some other reason behind wanting her to change. Stubborn; won't be reasonable. Group asks questions about other section heads; why don't they get on with her? What kind of person is she? How did Vic tell her to make changes? How did she act?
Analysis	What is she really trying to preserve? Is she afraid of something? If so, what? Are there people on those detailed jobs she depends on too much to let go? Would it mean salary cut? Does she think it would? Vic doesn't know.
Decision	Role-play situation next meeting, with Vic playing unreasonable section head. See if that gives clue to her actions and how Vic should handle situation.

Sample Structure and Content for a Recorder's Record

Subject	Action	Notes
Vic's Problem	Vic outlines situation as he sees it—what he wants to achieve and why. Vic still	Vic talking—group interested.
Facts and Obstacles	talking, describing all angles. Group begins asking questions.	Group still interested but growing restive. Several want to ask questions—hold back —finally break in.
	Gene asks what other section chiefs are like. Mac trying to find out what everybody does. Asks for organization chart. Gene back to section chiefs. Mac comes back to jobs. Norm asks has Vic talked to her about it? Vic explodes—*has he!* Edna finally breaks in; wants more dope on section chief as human being: what's she like? What's making her act this way? Mac and Gene arguing on side. Norm mediates. Jim asks Vic about Edna's questions.	Wandering all over the lot. Mac and Gene monopolizing questions. Why won't Mac stick to subject? Edna wants to get in her questions. Nobody giving her a chance. Somebody should stop this. Why doesn't the blackboard member bust it?
		Nice work, Norm and Jim.
	Vic repeats what he said before. Jim comes in with: Tell us more about how you handled it. Vic talks.	Group bored. Sitting it out now—3 min.–4.
Analysis	Norm again, bringing them back to Edna's questions. Getting below surface. Norm, Gene, Edna hypothesizing on reasons for section chief holding out. Interesting but not getting anywhere so far.	Norm helping Edna, trying to lead into analysis. Group is interested again; listening.
Solution	Jim suggests role-play at next meeting. Pause. Gene, okay. Edna, okay. Norm, okay. How about it, Vic? Sure. Planning details.	

(In starting the evaluation at the end of the meeting, the observer passed over all the notes given here except those showing poor member responsibility, and started group talking about that: how and why it had happened.)

Sample Post-Meeting Reaction Sheets and Summaries

Very simple post-meeting reaction sheets and summaries can show a group what difficulties are keeping down its production and how to help the members correct them.

Here is a form for a simple analysis sheet:

Sample of Simple Reaction Sheet

WHAT DO YOU THINK?

If you will answer the following questions, it will help us a great deal in improving our future meetings.

1. What did you think were the weaknesses in today's meeting?
2. What did you think were the strong points?
3. What improvements would you suggest in the operation of the next meeting?

Please date sheet but *do not sign* your name.

Following is a compilation of remarks made about a meeting on a simple post-meeting reaction sheet:

Sample Summary of Post-Meeting Reactions	*Times Mentioned*
1. What were the weak points in this meeting?	
Too much dependence on leader	2
Discussion not as lively as last week	2
Too much expression of opinion instead of trying to integrate ideas	1
Some members still too shy to participate	3
One or two members have tendency to dominate	4
Not enough progress on problem	1
Some wandering from subject	2
2. What were the strong points?	
Excellent interest	5
Good group interaction, members supporting each other	3
Good progress on problem	6
Ease of participation, relaxed atmosphere	4
Good leadership	1

Good job by blackboard member   1
3. Suggested improvements
   More balanced participation, group draw in quiet members   4
   Better ventilation   1
   Dominating members give others more chance   3
   Stay on subject   2

If members are willing to put in the compiling time necessary, they can work out more complicated devices and focus on almost any aspect of the meeting they wish. The next pair of samples are from a group which became very much interested in the process of what goes on in a group, and much concerned about weak participation.

Post-Meeting Reaction Sheet

(Date)_____

What did you think of this meeting? Please be frank. Your comments can contribute a great deal to our future meetings. You will receive a copy of the summary of all the comments.

1. What did you like about today's meeting?
2. What did you dislike?
3. What improvements would you suggest in the operation of the next meeting?
4. Of the times you wanted to talk but did not, how many were because—
   a. You couldn't break in when you wanted?   About _____ times
   b. On the whole it didn't seem worth while?   About _____ times
   c. The group might not accept the
      contribution well?   About _____ times
   d. It would not have helped the group at
      that moment?   About _____ times
   e. You couldn't phrase it well enough?   About _____ times
   f. Someone else said it?   About _____ times
   g. Reasons other than those listed here (please specify):
      _____   About _____ times
      _____   About _____ times
5. On the whole, how do you rate this meeting? (Check one.)

No good   Mediocre   All right   Good   Excellent

You do not need to sign your name.

In the following sample summary of the complex p.m.r. sheet just shown, the comments are grouped by different aspects of the meeting (listed as A, B, C, etc.). The likes and dislikes in each aspect are placed opposite each other so members can compare them easily. Each comment is listed separately. The suggested improvements and participation data follow the likes and dislikes.

Summary of Members' Post-Meeting Reactions

A. Purpose and Process

Likes	Dislikes
1. Agreement on problem of mutual interest helped unify group.	1. Didn't get enough specific points listed.
2. Matter to be discussed was decided quickly.	2. Wasn't interested in topic particularly.
3. Didn't take us long to choose a goal.	
4. A lot was accomplished.	
5. Moved toward goal.	
6. Progress was made on point at issue.	

B. Atmosphere and Attention

1. Those that did participate seemed interested.
2. Pace free.
3. Good humor of group.
4. Relaxed atmosphere by most members.
5. There seems to be a good spirit and ease in the group.
6. Silences when they occur are no longer uncomfortable.

C. Quality of Discussion

1. Good discussion by those who participated.	1. It seemed to be more difficult for most of the members to make suggestions on the points in question.
2. Thinking was stimulated to a very high degree.	2. Used many concepts and words without defining as well as needed for discussion.

Likes	*Dislikes*

3. I checked the meeting as "good" because I think it will be valuable to review the record.

3. Lack of clear thinking and expression.

4. Discussion flowed freely.

4. Not enough disagreement.

D. Pertinence of Discussion
1. Little straying from point under discussion.
2. We kept fairly well focused on the topic.
3. Attention constantly focused on main topic under discussion.
4. Not too much diversion in discussion, very little, in fact.

1. Occasional attempts to argue about irrelevant points or terms in light of over-all objective.

E. Group Development
1. Bill, realizing his responsibility as a group member, came to leader's assistance a few times.
2. There seemed to be a sincere effort to clarify our thinking —little distraction.
3. Group refused to be diverted into tangents.
5. Much interplay between members of the group.

1. People still forgetting their responsibilities as group members; I often did.

2. The group did not seem to be "together"—perhaps it was because of the nature of the topic discussed.

F. Leadership
1. Leader conscious of his responsibility as leader.

2. Continuity supported by leader.
3. Genial attitude of leader.
4. Ken did well as leader.
5. Leader keeping us on focus.
6. Leader asking the recorder for a summary.

1. Leader sometimes went too far in ascribing group's ideas to group.
2. Leader could have summarized better at times.

Likes	Dislikes
G. *Participation*	
1. Interest was good even though all did not participate verbally.	1. Some members did not participate.
2. Most people participated.	2. Almost no participation by some members.
	3. Some people who ordinarily participate did so hardly at all this evening.

SUGGESTED IMPROVEMENTS

A. *Pertinence of Discussion*
  1. That discussion be more focused.
B. *Group Development*
  1. Members be aware of their responsibility to keep discussion focused.
C. *Participation*
  1. Group should attempt to draw in nonverbal members.
  2. Attempt should be made to draw in nonparticipants.
  3. Silent members should take responsibility of expressing themselves if topic is vital to them; if not, of asking for change of topic.

FREQUENCY AND CAUSES OF WITHHELD COMMENTS

Reason	*Times Mentioned*
a. Couldn't break in.	12
b. Didn't seem worth while.	8
c. Might not be accepted well.	7
d. Would not have helped.	5
e. Couldn't phrase it properly.	2
f. Someone else said it.	2
g. Lack of confidence.	1
h. Waited for someone else.	4
i. Couldn't understand.	6

MEMBERS' RATING OF MEETING

Excellent	3
Good	7
All Right	2
Mediocre	—
No Good	—

APPENDIX II

TRAINING PLAN FOR
CONFERENCE LEADERSHIP TEAMS

The training schedule that follows fills a hard-working day, and each practice or explanatory session must begin and end promptly. The plan is a sample only, intended to be used as a guide, and adjusted to fit the size and needs of a particular conference. If yours is smaller than the one we have projected, fewer leadership teams and a less complex arrangement would do; if larger, more teams and a larger training staff are needed.

Whatever plan you use, give the delegates who will serve on the leadership teams some advance knowledge of what they will be doing. As soon as they have been picked, they should have information about their jobs: material prepared by the steering committee, or suggested reading.

The object throughout this day of training is to give practice in techniques. Subject matter for the practice meetings is important both for its content and to provide a vehicle for the leadership teams to learn their jobs and to learn to work together. As we mentioned before, you will need one large room and as many small rooms as there are leadership teams.

This sample plan is based on a conference of about two hundred delegates, for whom twelve leadership teams should be enough (in each group at the conference proper there will then be about twelve members besides the leadership team of four). Hence forty-eight of your delegates will arrive a day early for this training. They will be helped in all details of the practice sessions by an over-all training staff: a director (who is the leader of the training staff), a trainer for blackboard members, a trainer for recorders, and a trainer for observers—four in all. Although each of these has his special field in which to work in the early afternoon sessions, he is competent to help and direct any one of the leadership jobs, and does.

Here is the sample plan:

9:30–10:00 a.m. Registration and Assignment
   1. Registration of forty-eight delegates.

2. Assignment of forty-eight delegates to twelve teams of four members each. For convenience, we label the teams, A-1, A-2, A-3; B-1, B-2, B-3; C-1, C-2, C-3; D-1, D-2, D-3.
3. Assignment of teams to small rooms; each delegate given a schedule for the day, showing where he will be for each session, and the seating arrangements for the general meetings. For the opening session all delegates are assigned to the large meeting room with the leaders of the twelve teams on the platform.

10:00–10:30   Introduction and Demonstration
1. Director (leader of training staff) introduces himself and other three trainers. Each explains his function, i.e., the function of a leader, a blackboard member, a recorder, and an observer. Or the four may hold a joint discussion of their jobs. The reason for each job, how it promotes better production for any group, must be explained so that leadership teams understand the purpose of what they will be doing in the conference. Limit this to ten minutes.
2. Director (in his role of leader) holds a demonstration meeting with the leaders of the twelve teams already assembled on platform, seated in a semicircle, acting as group members. Other three trainers act as blackboard member, recorder, and observer.

Subject: What's Wrong with Most Meetings?
Limit to ten minutes. Though this sounds difficult, it has been done frequently. Given an opportunity, people quickly bring to light their pet gripes about meetings that have bored or frustrated them.
Trainer-observer gives one-minute report, leads group in evaluation. This should bring out examples of principles outlined by training staff in their introduction to the demonstration. Takes the final ten minutes of this half-hour.

10:30–11:00   Preparation for Practice Sessions
Director assigns to each team subject matter for practice meetings, each subject being how to prevent one of the faults listed in the demonstration meeting.
All A teams go to one small room with a member of the training staff. All B's to another, etc. Similar practice meetings will be going on in each room. (For simplicity we discuss only what occurs in one room.) Member of training staff with A teams and team members introduce themselves to each other. A-1 team gets together and makes plans for its practice meeting; A-2 and A-3 do the same in other parts of the room. Member of the training staff available for consultation.

11:00–12:00 *Practice Sessions*

Each team takes its turn at leading a practice meeting, ten minutes in length, with members of other teams serving as group members, discussing assigned subject. The recorder makes his record; the blackboard member does his chalking; the observer makes his notes. At the end of each practice meeting, the team observer reports for one minute and the group evaluates for about eight minutes, leaving a brief time for the group to adjust to a new subject and a new leadership team. Member of the training staff gives suggestions as needed.

12:00–1:00 *Lunch*

1:00–1:30 *Discussion of Separate Functions*

All leaders go to one room, recorders to a second, blackboard members to a third, and observers to a fourth. The appropriate member of the training staff goes with each group. Each trainer leads his group in a discussion of its functions, and the members compile a list of guides for their activity in the conference (which the staff reproduces and distributes later).

1:40–3:30 *Second Set of Practice Meetings*

The teams are shuffled for the afternoon's practice meetings so that each team leads a group different from the one it worked with in the morning:

Room W	Room X	Room Y	Room Z
Teams A-1	Teams B-1	Teams C-1	Teams D-1
B-2	A-2	D-2	C-2
C-3	D-3	A-3	B-3

After twenty minutes in which each team meets separately to plan for the meeting it will conduct, the teams rotate the leading of practice meetings, as they did in the morning session. This time, however, each meeting lasts for twenty minutes before the one-minute report from the team observer and seven- or eight-minute evaluation by the group. As in the morning, the staff member participates to clear up misunderstandings.

Subject matter: Two of the teams in each room lead discussions on problems which groups will work on at the conference proper. The third team's subject is: What is the best way to introduce this type of conference to the delegates at the opening session? (A prearranged skit showing "Two Kinds of Meetings," or "One Good Meeting," or a four-way discussion by the training staff, are among the possibilities.) Discussing specific problems the small groups will work on the next day has the advantage of giving the teams' members a more lifelike dress rehearsal for their jobs. Being able to help determine how to open the conference makes it more "their conference," increases their feeling of participation.

3:30–3:45   Break

From 3:45   Summing Up

After the afternoon break the team members come back to meet together in the large meeting room. Four teams, one chosen by lot (or volunteering) from each group, are on the platform to discuss the recommendations of the meetings which considered the opening of the conference, and to decide how it is to be done. The leadership team for the session has also been chosen by lot from among the four. Since this is the last scheduled meeting of the day, it can be as long as the problem requires, or as short as the team members' remaining energy permits.

If the decision is to open the conference with some type of role-playing, the members who volunteer to do it will need some time afterward, or in the evening, to make their plans and, if they wish, try a quick practice session.

Later Meetings of Leadership Teams

Meetings of leadership team members during the course of the conference can be very helpful. Problems come up during the meetings which could not be anticipated (or indeed recognized) by the team members until they are experienced in the reality of the actual discussions. These extra meetings make it possible for the leaders to share the problems they have encountered, and what solutions any of them have found. The observers can share theirs similarly. Meetings of recorders and of blackboard members can serve the same purposes.

SELECTED READING LIST

ACCOMPLISHING CHANGE

1. Beckhard, Richard. *The Leader Looks at the Consultative Process.* Washington, D.C.: Leadership Resources, Inc., 1961.
2. Benne, Kenneth D., Bradford, Leland P., and Lippitt, Ronald. "Group Dynamics and Social Action." New York: Anti-Defamation League of the B'nai B'rith, 1950.
3. Bennett, T. R. *The Leader Looks at the Process of Change.* Washington, D.C.: Leadership Resources, Inc., 1961.
4. Bennis, Warren G., Benne, Kenneth D., and Chin, R. (eds.). *The Planning of Change.* New York: Holt, Rinehart & Winston, 1961.
5. Cartwright, Dorwin. "Achieving Change in People," in *Human Relations*, Vol. 2, 1949.
6. ——. *Studies in Social Power.* Ann Arbor: University of Michigan, 1959.
7. Coch, L. and French, J. "Overcoming Resistance to Change," in *Human Relations*, Vol. 1, #4, 1948.
8. Ginzberg, Eli and Reilley, E. W. *Effecting Change in Large Organizations.* New York: Columbia University Press, 1957.
9. Jaques, Elliott. *The Changing Culture of a Factory.* London: Tavistock Publications, 1951.
10. Johnson, Wendell. "The Fateful Process of Mr. A. Talking to Mr. B," in *Harvard Business Review*, Vol. XXXI, #1, 1953.
11. Leighton, A. H. *The Governing of Men.* Princeton: Princeton University Press, 1945.
12. Lewin, Kurt. *Resolving Social Conflicts.* New York: Harper, 1948.
13. Lippitt, Ronald, and others. *Dynamics of Planned Change.* New York: Harcourt, Brace, 1958.
14. Mann, F. C. and Neff, F. W. *Managing Major Change in Organizations.* Ann Arbor: Foundation for Research on Human Behavior, 1961.
15. Mann, F. C. "Studying and Creating Change: A Means to Understanding Social Behavior," in C. M. Arensburg and others, *Research in Industrial Human Relations.* New York: Harper, 1957.
16. Merei, F. "Group Leadership and Institutionalization," in *Human Relations*, Vol. 4, 1951.
17. Poston, R. W. *Democracy Is You.* New York: Harper, 1953. University Press, 1957.
18. Sofer, Cyril. *The Organization from Within.* London: Tavistock Publications, 1961.
19. Cumming, E. and J. H. *Closed Ranks.* Cambridge, Mass.: Harvard

20. Jenkins, D. H., and Lippitt, R. *Interpersonal Perceptions of Teachers, Students and Parents.* Research Training Action Series, #1. Washington, D.C.: National Education Association, 1951.
21. Marrow, Alfred J. *Changing Patterns of Prejudice.* Philadelphia: Chilton Company, 1962.

COMMUNICATION AND ACTION
1. Barnlund, Dean C. and Haiman, F. S. *Dynamics of Discussion.* Boston: Houghton, Mifflin, 1960.
2. Hall, Edward T. *The Silent Language.* New York: Doubleday, 1959.
3. Haney, William V. *Communication: Patterns and Incidents.* Homewood, Ill.: Richard Irwin, 1960.
4. Johnson, Wendell. "The Fateful Process of Mr. A. Talking to Mr. B.," op. cit.
5. Lee, Irving. *Handling Barriers in Communication.* New York: Harpers, 1957.
6. Leighton, A. H. *Human Relations in a Changing World.* New York: Dutton, 1949.
7. Pigors, Paul. *Effective Communication in Industry.* New York: National Association of Manufacturers, 1949.
8. Redfield, Charles E. *Communication in Management.* Chicago: University of Chicago Press, 1953.
9. Rogers, C. R. and Roethlisberger, F. J. "Barriers and Gateways to Communication," in *Harvard Business Review,* July-August, 1952.
10. Schmidt, W. and Buchanan, P. *Techniques That Produce Teamwork.* New London, Conn.: National Foremen's Institute, 1954.
11. Thayer, Lee O. *Administrative Communication.* Homewood, Ill.: Richard Irwin, 1961.
12. This, Leslie. *The Leader Looks at Communication.* Washington, D.C.: Leadership Resources, Inc., 1961.

COMMUNITY DEVELOPMENT
1. Abrahamson, Julia. *A Neighborhood Finds Itself.* New York: Harper, 1959.
2. Biddle, William W. *Cultivation of Community Leaders.* New York: Harper, 1953.
3. Brownell, Baker. *Human Community.* New York: Harper, 1950.
4. Coleman, James S. *Community Conflict.* New York: Macmillan, 1957.
5. Hillman, Arthur. *Community Organization and Planning.* New York: Macmillan, 1950.
6. Hunter, Floyd. *Community Power Structure.* Chapel Hill, N.C.: University of North Carolina Press, 1953.

7. Mial, Dorothy and H. Curtis (eds.). *Our Community*. New York: New York University Press, 1960.
8. ———. *Forces in Community Development*. Washington, D.C.: National Training Laboratories, National Educational Association, 1961.
9. Nelson, Lowry, and others. *Community Structure and Change*. New York: Macmillan, 1960.
10. Ross, Murray G. *Community Organization*. New York: Harper, 1955.
11. Sanders, I. T. *The Community*. New York: The Ronald Press, 1958.
12. Sower, Christopher, and others. *Community Involvement*. Glencoe, Ill.: Free Press, 1957.
13. Sherif, Muzafer (ed.). *Intergroup Relations and Leadership*. New York: Wiley, 1962.
14. Warren, Roland L. *Studying Your Community*. New York: Russell Sage Foundation, 1955.
15. ———. *The Community Self-Study Process*. Hempstead, L.I., N.Y.: Hofstra College, 1958.

CONFERENCES AND WORKSHOPS

1. Adult Education Association of the United States. *Conducting Workshops and Institutes*. Chicago: Leadership Pamphlet #9, 1958.
2. ———. *Conferences That Work*. Chicago: Leadership Pamphlet #11, 1959.
3. Bales, Robert F. "In Conference," *Harvard Business Review*, Vol. XXXII, #2, March-April, 1954.
4. Beckhard, Richard (ed.). *Conferences for Learning, Planning and Action*. Washington, D.C.: National Training Laboratories, National Education Association, 1962.
5. ———. *How to Plan and Conduct Workshops and Conferences*. New York: Association Press, 1956.
6. Maier, Norman R. F. *Problem-Solving Discussion and Conferences: Leadership Methods and Skills*. New York: McGraw-Hill, 1963.
7. National Training Laboratories. *Conference Planning*. Washington, D.C.: Selected Reading Series #6, 1962.
8. Schmidt, W. and Beckhard, Richard. *The Fact Finding Conference*. Chicago: Adult Education Association of the United States, 1956.
9. "A Tale of Three Conferences," *Adult Education Bulletin*, February 1948. Washington, D.C.: National Education Association.
10. "A Thousand Think Together," New York: National Nursing Council, 1948.

LEADERSHIP

1. Argyris, Chris. *Interpersonal Competence and Organizational Effectiveness*. Homewood, Ill.: Richard Irwin, 1962.

2. Beal, George M., and others. *Leadership and Dynamic Group Action.* Ames: Iowa State University Press, 1962.
3. Bennett, T. R. *The Leader and the Process of Change.* New York: Association Press, 1960.
4. Gordon, Thomas. *Group-Centered Leadership.* Boston: Houghton, Mifflin, 1955.
5. Jennings, Eugene E. *An Anatomy of Leadership.* New York: Harper, 1960.
6. Knowles, Malcolm S. and Knowles, H. F. *How to Develop Better Leaders.* New York: Association Press, 1955.
7. Lippitt, Gordon L. (ed.). *Leadership in Action.* Washington, D.C.: National Training Laboratories, National Education Association, 1961.
8. Lynton, R. P. *The Tide of Learning—The Aloka Experience.* London: Routledge & Kegan Paul, 1960.
9. Petrullo, Luigi and Bass, B. M. *Leadership and Interpersonal Behavior.* New York: Holt, Rinehart & Winston, 1961.
10. Ross, M. G. and Hendry, C. E. *New Understandings of Leadership.* New York: Association Press, 1957.
11. Schmidt, W. R. *The Leader Looks at the Leadership Dilemma.* Washington, D.C.: Leadership Resources, Inc., 1961.
12. Tannenbaum, Robert, and others. *Leadership and Organization, A Behavioral Science Approach.* New York: McGraw-Hill, 1961.
13. White, Ralph K. and Lippitt, Ronald. *Autocracy and Democracy: An Experimental Inquiry.* New York: Harper, 1960.
14. Bass, Bernard M. *Leadership, Psychology and Organizational Behavior.* New York: Harper and Row, 1960.
15. Dalton, Melville. *Men Who Manage.* New York: Wiley, 1959.

MOTIVATION AND GROWTH

1. Baller, Warren R. *Readings in the Psychology of Human Growth and Development.* New York: Holt, Rinehart & Winston, 1962.
2. Buchanan, P. C. *The Leader Looks at Individual Motivation.* Washington, D.C.: Leadership Resources, Inc., 1961.
3. Jahoda, Marie. "Current Concepts of Positive Mental Health," in *The Psychological Meaning of Various Criteria for Positive Mental Health.* New York: Basic Books, 1958.
4. Knowles, Malcolm S. *The Leader Looks at Self-Development.* Washington, D.C.: Leadership Resources, Inc., 1961.
5. Leighton, A. H. *Human Relations in a Changing World.* New York: Dutton, 1949.
6. Rogers, Carl R. *On Becoming a Person.* Boston: Houghton, Mifflin, 1961.

7. Weschler, I. R. *The Leader Looks at Creativity.* Washington, D.C.: Leadership Resources, Inc., 1961.
8. Whyte, William F., and others. *Money and Motivation.* New York: Harper, 1955.
9. Combs, A. W. (ed.). *Perceiving, Behaving, Becoming.* Washington, D.C.: National Education Association, 1962.

ORGANIZATION AND MANAGEMENT

1. Argyris, Chris. *The Impact of Budgets on People.* Ithaca, N. Y.: Cornell University, 1952.
2. ———. *Personality and Organization.* New York: Harper, 1957.
3. ———. *Understanding Organizational Behavior.* Homewood, Ill.: Richard Irwin, 1960.
4. Blake, Robert and Mouton, Jane. *Group Dynamics: Key to Decision Making.* Houston: Gulf Publishing Co., 1961.
5. Blansfield, M. G. *The Leader Looks at Appraisal of Personnel.* Washington, D.C.: Leadership Resources, Inc., 1961.
6. Brown, David S. *The Leader Looks at Authority and Hierarchy.* Washington, D.C.: Leadership Resources, Inc., 1961.
7. ———. *The Leader Looks at Decision Making.* Washington, D.C.: Leadership Resources, Inc., 1961.
8. Chapple, E. D., and Sayles, L. R. *The Measure of Management.* New York: Macmillan, 1961.
9. Davis, Keith. *Human Relations at Work.* New York: McGraw-Hill, 1962.
10. Drucker, Peter. *The Practice of Management.* New York: Harper, 1954.
11. Dubin, Robert. *Human Relations in Administration* (2nd ed.). Englewood Cliffs, N. J.: Prentice-Hall, 1961.
12. ———. *The World of Work.* Englewood Cliffs, N. J.: Prentice-Hall, 1958.
13. Haire, Mason. *Modern Organization Theory.* New York: Wiley, 1959.
14. ———. *Organization Theory and Industrial Practice.* New York: Wiley, 1962.
15. Lawrence, Paul R. *The Changing of Organizational Behavior Patterns.* Cambridge, Mass.: Harvard University Press, 1958.
16. Leavitt, Harold J. *Managerial Psychology.* Chicago: University of Chicago Press, 1958.
17. Lesieur, F. G. *The Scanlon Plan.* New York: Wiley, 1958.
18. Likert, Rensis. *New Patterns of Management.* New York: McGraw-Hill, 1961.
19. MacGregor, Douglas. *The Human Side of Enterprise.* New York: McGraw-Hill, 1960.

20. Mailick, Sidney and Van Ness, E. H. (eds.). *Concepts and Issues in Administrative Behavior*. Englewood Cliffs, N. J.: Prentice-Hall, 1962.
21. Maier, Norman R. F. and Hayes, J. J. *Creative Management*. New York: Wiley, 1962.
22. Melman, S. *Decision Making and Productivity*. Oxford, England: Basil Blackwell, 1958.
23. Merrihue, Willard V. *Managing by Communication*. New York: McGraw-Hill, 1960.
24. Pigors, Paul and Myers, Charles. *Personnel Administration* (4th ed.). New York: McGraw-Hill, 1961.
25. Pollock, Ross. *The Leader Looks at Appraisal of Personnel*. Washington, D.C.: Leadership Resources, Inc., 1961.
26. Scott, William G. *Human Relations in Management*. Homewood, Ill.: Richard Irwin, 1962.
27. Seckler-Hudson, Catheryn. *Organization and Management: Theory and Practice*. Washington, D.C.: American University Press, 1955.
28. Simon, H. A. *Administrative Behavior*. New York: Macmillan, 1957.
29. Smith, George A. *Managing Geographically Decentralized Companies*. Cambridge, Mass.: Harvard University Press, 1958.
30. Strauss, George and Sayles, Leonard. *Personnel: The Human Problems of Management*. Englewood Cliffs, N. J.: Prentice-Hall, 1960.
31. Walker, Charles R. and Walker, A. G. *Modern Technology and Civilization*. New York: McGraw-Hill, 1962.
32. Whyte, William F. *Man and Organization*. Homewood, Ill.: Richard Irwin, 1959.
33. ———. *Men at Work*. Homewood, Ill.: Richard Irwin, 1961.
34. Zaleznik, Abraham, and others. *The Motivation, Productivity, and Satisfaction of Workers*. Cambridge, Mass.: Harvard University Graduate School of Business Administration, 1958.

ROLE PLAYING

1. Adult Education Association of the United States. *How to Use Role Playing and Other Tools for Learning*. Chicago: Leadership Pamphlet #6, 1957.
2. Argyris, Chris. *Role Playing in Action*. Ithaca, N.Y.: New York State School of Industrial and Labor Relations, Cornell University, 1951.
3. French, J. R. P. "Retraining an Autocratic Leader," *Journal of Abnormal and Social Psychology*, Vol. 39, #2, April 1944.
4. Hendry, C. E., Lippitt, Ronald, and Zander, A. "Reality Practice as Educational Method." *Psychodrama Monograph No. 9*. Beacon, N.Y.: Beacon House, 1944.
5. Klein, Alan F. *How To Use Role Playing Effectively*. New York: Association Press, 1951.

6. ——. *Role Playing in Leadership Training and Group Problem Solving.* New York: Association Press, 1956.
7. Lippitt, Ronald. "The Psychodrama in Leadership Training." *Sociometry,* Vol. I, No. 3, 1943.
8. Maier, Norman R. F. *Principles of Human Relations.* New York: Wiley, 1957.
9. Maier, Norman R. F., and others. *Supervisory and Executive Development: A Manual for Role Playing.* New York: Wiley, 1957.
10. O'Donnell, W. G. "Role Playing as a Practical Training Technique," in *Personnel,* New York: American Management Association, November 1952.

SMALL GROUP BEHAVIOR

1. Adult Education Association of the United States. *Understanding How Groups Work.* Chicago: Leadership Pamphlet #4, 1956.
2. Bales, Robert F. *Interaction Process Analysis.* Cambridge, Mass.: Addison-Wesley, 1950.
3. Bradford, Leland P. (ed.). *Group Development.* Washington, D.C.: National Training Laboratories, National Education Association, 1961.
4. Cartwright, Dorwin and Zander, A. F. *Group Dynamics, Theory and Research.* Evanston, Ill.: Row, Peterson, 1953.
5. "Dynamics of the Discussion Group," *Journal of Social Issues,* Vol. IV, No. 2. New York: Association Press, 1948.
6. Festinger, Leon, and others. *Social Pressures in Informed Groups.* New York: Harper, 1950.
7. Hare, A. P. *Handbook of Small Group Research.* Glencoe, Ill.: Free Press, 1962.
8. Hare, A. P., and others (eds.). *Small Groups, Studies in Social Interaction.* New York: Knopf, 1955.
9. Homans, George C. *The Human Group.* New York: Harcourt, Brace, 1950.
10. Jennings, Helen H. *Sociometry in Group Relations.* Washington, D.C.: American Council on Education, 1959.
11. Klein, Josephine. *Working with Groups: The Social Psychology of Discussion and Decision.* London: Hutchinson, 1961.
12. Lee, Irving. *How To Talk with People.* New York: Harper, 1952.
13. Lifton, Walter M. *Working with Groups.* New York: Wiley, 1961.
14. Lippitt, G. L. and Whitfield, E. *The Leader Looks at Group Effectiveness.* Washington, D.C.: Leadership Resources, Inc., 1961.
15. Maccoby, Eleanor E., and others. *Readings in Social Psychology.* New York: Holt, 1958.

16. Newcomb, T. M. "Group Solidarity," in *Social Psychology*. New York: Dryden Press, 1950.
17. Olmsted, Michael. *The Small Group*. New York: Random House, 1959.
18. Proctor, C. H. and Loomis, C. P. "Analysis of Sociometric Data" in *Research Methods in Social Relations*. Ed. by Marie Jahoda, and others. New York: Dryden Press, 1951.
19. Thibaut, John W. and Kelley, H. H. *The Social Psychology of Groups*. New York: Wiley, 1959.
20. Trist, E. L. and Sofer, Cyril. *Exploration in Group Relations*. Leicester, England: Leicester University Press, 1959.
21. Whyte, William F. "Leadership and Group Participation," in New York State School of Industrial Relations' Bulletin #24. Ithaca, N.Y.: Cornell University, May 1953.
22. ———. *Street Corner Society*. Chicago: University of Chicago Press, 1943.
23. Wilson, Donald P. *My Six Convicts*. New York: Rinehart, 1951.
24. Bell, Earl H. *Social Foundations of Human Behavior*. New York: Harper and Row, 1961.
25. Homans, G. C. *Social Behavior*. New York: Harcourt, Brace and World, 1961.
26. Knowles, M. S. and H. F. *Introduction to Group Dynamics*. New York: Association Press, 1959.

TRAINING

1. Adult Education Association of the United States. *Training Group Leaders*. Chicago: Leadership Pamphlet #8, 1958.
2. ———. *Training in Human Relations*. Chicago: Leadership Pamphlet #16, 1959.
3. Agency for International Development. *Conference Training Leadership*. Washington, D.C.: Technical Bulletin #21.
4. ———. *Discussion Leadership*. Washington, D.C.: Technical Bulletin #12.
5. Batten, Thomas R. *Training for Community Development*. London: Oxford University Press, 1962.
6. Berlo, David K. *The Process of Communication*. New York: Holt, Rinehart & Winston, 1960.
7. Bradford, Leland P. (ed.). *Human Forces in Teaching and Learning*. Washington, D.C.: National Training Laboratories, National Education Association, 1959.
8. Cantor, Nathaniel F. *The Learning Process for Managers*. New York: Harper, 1958.

9. Kelley, Earl C. *The Workshop Way of Learning.* New York: Harper, 1951.
10. Lippitt, Ronald. *Training in Community Relations.* New York: Harper, 1949.
11. Miles, Matthew B. *Learning to Work in Groups.* New York: Columbia University Press, 1959.
12. National Training Laboratories. *Communication, Leadership, Problem Solving and Productivity.* Training Workbook #5. Washington, D.C.: National Education Association, 1958.
13. ———. *Forces in Learning.* Selected Reading Series #3. Washington, D.C.: National Education Association, 1961.
14. ———. *Group Observation and Recording.* Training Workbook #1. Washington, D.C.: National Education Association, 1958.
15. ———. *Issues in Training.* Selected Reading Series #5. Washington, D.C.: National Education Association, 1962.
16. ———. *Sample Group Evaluation Forms.* Training Workbook #2. Washington, D.C.: National Education Association, 1958.
17. Wiles, Kimball. *Supervision for Better Schools.* New York: Prentice-Hall, 1950.

SENSITIVITY TRAINING
1. Marrow, Alfred J. *Behind the Executive Desk.* New York: American Management Association. 1964.

INDEX

Agendas: one-meeting group and, 102; shaping of, 40–42

All-at-once introduction, 36–38; dress rehearsal for, 36–37; preliminary talk in, 36

"Always Vulnerable" behavior type, 13

Analysis: group, 85–89; observer's sheet and, 87; short cuts for, 131–133; situation, 97–100

Behavior types, 10–14, 75–82

"Belittler" behavior type, 13, 82

Blackboard member, 17, 27–30; activity of, 42; choice of, 111; dress rehearsal for, 36–37; leader as, 102; in one-meeting group, 102; in "working conference," 110–13

"Blocker" behavior type, 13–14, 81

Bradford, Leland, 57

"Brainstorming," 48

Buzz groups, 51; for comment, 57; effectiveness of, 51–52; for information, 57; large meetings and, 54–58; leadership in, 119; lectures and, 55–56; listening teams and, 57–58; at Monze, 151, 153; problem solving and, 47; small meetings and, 51–54; as stimulant, 56–57; uses of, 52–57; in worker-centered meetings, 130; in "working conferences," 116, 117, 118

Chairmen: member-centered meetings and, 15–27; problems types and, 14 (see also Leaders)

Change: stimulating, 94–100

Committees: Lambs-to-Slaughter (see Lambs-to-Slaughter Committees; Railroaded (see Railroaded Committees)

Communication, 124; directives as, 130; "highly effective group" and, 125–26; leaflets as, 130; mobility of,

129–31; of policy, 130; suggestion box as, 127–29

Conferences, working (see "Working conferences")

Conformity, problem of, 120

Decisions, delegate-made, 105

"Depreciator" behavior type, 12

Destructive types, 12; always vulnerable, 13; belittler, 13, 81–82; blocker, 13–14, 81; distractor, 14, 81–82; dominator, 13, 80–81; handling of, 80–83; manipulator, 13, 82; new member, 82; saboteur, 82–83; talker, 11, 81

"Distractor" behavior type, 14, 81–82

"Dominator" behavior type, 13, 80–81

"Doubting Thomas" behavior type, 12

"Eager Beaver" behavior type, 10, 76–77

Easel member see Blackboard member

Evaluation, 83, 157; example of, 37, 39; of leaders, 37; of meetings, 31–33; in one-meeting groups, 104; of role-playing, 71–72

Executives, 118; member-centered meetings and, 118–19; selection of, 139–43

"Exercises," 60 (see also Role-playing)

Experts: use of, 89–94; at "working conference," 109–10

"Explorer" behavior type, 11, 76

"Feeler letters," 105

"Fence-sitter" behavior type, 11–12, 76–77

Gordon, K., 20n.

Groups: analysis of, 85–89; buzz (see Buzz groups); community (see Community groups); differences in, 9–10; "highly effective," 125–26; member-centered meetings and, 1–

177